Looking at Type: The Fundamentals

by Charles R. Martin, Ph.D.

CENTER FOR APPLICATIONS OF PSYCHOLOGICAL TYPE, INC.

GAINESVILLE, FLORIDA

Published by
Center for Applications of
Psychological Type, Inc.
2815 NW 13th Street, Suite 401
Gainesville, FL 32609
(352) 375-0160

Edited by Nancy T. Savage and
Jamelyn R. DeLong

The publisher gratefully acknowledges the assistance of Production Ink, Gainesville, Florida, for the design, production, and printing of this title.

Printed in the United States of America.

ISBN 0-935652-31-0

Acknowledgments

This book has come into being through the generous input and support of countless people in my personal life and professional life. Friends, family, colleagues, workshop participants, and clients have all taught me much and have contributed to the content of this work.

I would like to thank Scott Anchors, Jamelyn DeLong, Larry Demarest, Tom Golatz, Dan Robinson, and other colleagues for their thoughtful and very helpful reviews of the manuscript. Appreciation goes to both Mary McCaulley and Gordon Lawrence from whom I have learned so much about type. Both have carried forward the work begun so many years ago by Isabel Myers. Special appreciation goes to Jerry Macdaid, who continually discusses with me some of the finer points of type, and whose ideas and input have contributed to the development of this book.

Finally, heartfelt thanks go to my wife and daughter for the love, wisdom, and joy they continually bring into my life.

Contents

Introduction

A common experience in people's lives is that they notice how their families, friends, and coworkers do not experience or view the world as they do. This book describes a model of personality that gives us insight into how and why people understand and approach the world in such different ways. As you are introduced to the different personality preferences described herein, you will no doubt recognize them in your own life, the gifts each preference brings to human life, and the blind spots if they are ignored.

This book is designed to accompany an explanation of a questionnaire, the Myers-Briggs Type Indicator®, also referred to as the "MBTI®" or "the Indicator." The Indicator provides a useful way of describing people's personalities by looking at their preferences on four scales (extraversion vs. introversion, sensing vs. intuition, thinking vs. feeling, and judging vs. perceiving), preferences which combine to yield one of sixteen different types. There are no right or wrong answers to the questions on the MBTI, just as there are no right or wrong types. In fact, all types are good types!

Looking at Type: The Fundamentals is the introductory book in a series of books about the sixteen psychological types indicated by the MBTI. This book describes the basics of type, gives an introduction to type dynamics, provides in-depth descriptions of the sixteen types, and gives general applications of type ideas. Other books in the series focus on specific applications, such as the uses of type in careers or in organizations.

This book can be read without answering the Indicator. However, taking the Indicator can help you clarify your own preferences. One of the best ways to begin understanding type is to understand your own preferences— the way in which *you* see the world. Weigh what you read in this book and decide how it applies to your own life. Then use your understanding to see how other types look at life in ways that are different from your own.

Some readers prefer to go through the book in the order in which it is written. Others prefer to jump ahead to find the description of the type they came out on the Indicator. Later they read to find out where type comes from or how it is put to practical use. Choose the path that works best for you.

We hope this book opens an exciting door to type for you now, and provides the foundation for a deeper understanding in the future, to achieve the goal of Isabel Briggs Myers— "the constructive use of differences."

Mary H. McCaulley, Ph.D.
President
Center for Applications of
Psychological Type (CAPT)

History of the MBTI

The Myers-Briggs Type Indicator was developed by Isabel Briggs Myers and her mother, Katharine Cook Briggs. Their aim was to create a tool to indicate, validate, and put to practical use C. G. Jung's work on psychological types. Jung (1875–1961) was a Swiss psychiatrist whose book *Psychological Types* was an outgrowth of his efforts to understand individual differences among people.

Katharine Cook Briggs (1875–1968) and her daughter, Isabel Briggs Myers (1897–1980) encountered Jung's ideas in 1923 and began two decades of "type watching." During World War II, Myers decided that people could make better career choices and more constructive uses of differences between people if they knew about Jung's types. To that end Myers began creating a paper-and-pencil questionnaire to assess type. The Indicator was developed through several different versions over three decades as research was collected on thousands of people.

In 1975, Consulting Psychologists Press began publishing the MBTI for applied uses. In that same year, Isabel Myers and Mary McCaulley founded the Center for Applications of Psychological Type (CAPT), a nonprofit organization created to continue research on the Indicator and to provide training and education on type and the MBTI.

Since the MBTI's publication, applications of and research on type have exploded. In the past few years books and articles have been published relating type to careers, intimate relationships, counseling, parenting, children, business, teamwork, leadership, education, and spirituality. In 1976, the CAPT bibliography of the MBTI included 337 references. In 1997, there were over 5,600 references, and the list continues to grow.

In all applications of the MBTI, the emphasis is on understanding valuable differences between people. Knowing type not only helps you appreciate your own strengths, gifts, and potential growth edges, but also helps you understand and appreciate how and why others may differ from you. Knowing that these differences are all valuable can truly lead to more constructive communication and relationships.

The Indicator is now being used internationally. It has been translated into over two dozen languages and is used on every continent. People are continuing to discover that type is a powerful way to understand individual differences and that the Indicator is a sophisticated tool for practical applications of type.

What Are Type Preferences?

To begin making use of type, one must understand a basic concept: type preferences. These preferences are the building blocks for the sixteen types that will be discussed later.

Type is about *psychological* preferences. These preferences, however, are not as simple as whether we prefer the color red or the color blue. Rather, they represent consistent and enduring patterns of how we use our minds. The preferences can also be understood as opposite but related ways of using our minds, with the opposites being two halves that make up a whole—like front and back, for example.

In the type system, you report preferences on four scales, and each of these four scales has two halves.

To better grasp the idea of preferences, try the following exercise. On a separate piece of paper or in the margin of this booklet, write your name. Now, put the pen or pencil in your other hand and write your name again. How would you describe the differences between the two experiences? Did they *feel* different? Are there differences in the *quality* of the writing?

Some adjectives people use to contrast the two experiences are: easy-hard, comfortable-awkward, effortless-concentrated, natural-unnatural, and fast-slow. Others report differences in quality. Many people say that the writing with the nondominant hand looks very childlike and immature. Some people report that it was an interesting challenge, but not a challenge they would like to take on all day, every day. You certainly *could* give more attention to writing with your non-dominant hand, but it would take time and effort to become as comfortable with it as you are with your dominant hand.

There are important parallels to the psychological type preferences here. When people engage in everyday behaviors that call on their type preferences, they tend to feel natural, comfortable, confident, and competent. In contrast, when people engage in behaviors that call on their nonpreferences, they tend to feel unnatural, uncomfortable, less confident, and less competent. Often people will try to find ways around or avoid doing things that call on their nonpreferences.

Everyone uses both sides of any given preference pair, but they tend to rely on one side more than the other. Since we do not use both preferences of a pair at the same time, we get in the habit of using one more often and are usually much better at one than the other. As a result, our nonpreferences tend to be less developed and less trusted, although we still have and use them.

With practice, people can develop greater confidence and competence in their type nonpreferences. However, it does take energy and effort to learn to use them, just as it would to learn to write with your non-dominant hand. Also, because people tend to feel so much more comfortable, natural, and confident when they use their preferences, they typically do not like to use their non-preferences for extended periods! As a result, they always tend to have more comfort and skill in their preferences.

The Exercise of Preferences Leads to Differences Among Individuals

As we act on our type preferences, our behavior and personality come to reflect our unique approach to the world and to relationships. In short, our personality type grows out of our exercising our type preferences. From a type perspective, there are no good or bad preferences; having different preferences simply leads to people having different interests,

different ways of behaving, and different ways of viewing the world. People who have different type preferences also tend to have different strengths and potential areas of needed growth. Knowing this can help us appreciate the unique contributions each of us brings to the world.

In the following section, you will find descriptions of the basic type preferences. The four preference scales are:

Extraversion (E) or Introversion (I):
How do you direct your energy and attention?

Sensing (S) or Intuition (N*):
How do you prefer to take in information?

Thinking (T) or Feeling (F):
How do you prefer to make decisions?

Judging (J) or Perceiving (P):
How do you orient to the outer world?

As you read the descriptions that follow, ask yourself: which side of the preference pair seems more natural, effortless, and comfortable for me?

---

* N is used to represent Intuition so it is not confused with Introversion.

The Preferences

Extraversion and Introversion

The first type preference pair asks: what is the direction of your energy and attention? Do you more naturally turn to the outer world of people and things (extraversion), or to the inner world of ideas and images (introversion)? This preference is also referred to as your *attitude*.

Extraversion (E)

Key words:

outer world ▪ people ▪ action ▪ breadth

People who prefer extraversion are energized by active involvement in events, and they like to be immersed in a breadth of activities. They are most excited when they are around people, and they often have an energizing effect on those around them. When you are extraverting you like to move into action and to make things happen— extraverts usually feel very at home in the world. With their orientation to the outer world, extraverts often find their understanding of a problem becomes clearer if they can talk out loud about it and hear what others have to say.

People who prefer extraversion may:
▪ be seen as "go-getters" or "people-persons"
▪ feel comfortable with and like working in groups
▪ have a wide range of acquaintances and friends
▪ *sometimes* jump too quickly into activity and not allow enough time for reflection
▪ *sometimes* forget to pause to clarify the ideas that give aim or meaning to their activities

Introversion (I)

Key words:

inner world ▪ ideas ▪ reflection ▪ depth

People who prefer introversion are energized and excited when they are involved with the ideas, images, memories, and reactions that are a part of their inner world. Introverts often prefer solitary activities or spending time with one or two others with whom they feel an affinity, and they often have a calming effect on those around them. When you are introverting, you take time to reflect on ideas that explain the outer world —introverts like to have a clear idea of what they will be doing when they move into action. With their orientation to the inner world, introverts truly like the idea of something, often better than the something itself, and ideas are almost solid things for them.

People who prefer introversion may:
▪ be seen as calm and "centered" or reserved
▪ feel comfortable being alone and like solitary activities
▪ prefer fewer, more intense relationships
▪ *sometimes* spend too much time reflecting and not move into action quickly enough
▪ *sometimes* forget to check with the outside world to see if their ideas really fit their experience

Sensing and Intuition

This second type preference pair describes the way you like to take in information and what kind of information you tend to trust the most. In other words, what kind of *perception* do you prefer to use? Do you give more weight to information that comes in through your five senses (sensing), or do you give more weight to information that comes into your awareness by way of insight and imagination (intuition)?

Sensing (S)

Key words:

facts ▪ details ▪ experience ▪ present

People who have a preference for sensing are immersed in the ongoing richness of sensory experience and thus seem more grounded in everyday physical reality. They tend to be concerned with what is actual, present, current, and real. As they exercise their preference for sensing, they approach situations with an eye to the facts. Thus, they often develop a good memory for detail, become accurate in working with data, and remember facts or aspects of events that did not even seem relevant at the time they occurred. Sensing types are often good at seeing the practical applications of ideas and things, and may learn best when they can first see the pragmatic side of what is being taught. For sensing types, experience speaks louder than words or theory.

People who prefer sensing may:
▪ recall events as snapshots of what literally happened
▪ solve problems by working through things thoroughly for a precise understanding
▪ be pragmatic and look to the "bottom line"
▪ work from the facts to the big picture
▪ put experience first and place less trust in words and symbols
▪ *sometimes* focus so much on the facts of the present or past that they miss new possibilities

Intuition (N)

Key words:

symbols ▪ pattern ▪ theory ▪ future

People who have a preference for intuition are immersed in their impressions of the meanings or patterns in their experiences. They would rather gain understanding through insight than through hands-on experience. Intuitive types tend to be concerned with what is possible and new, and they have an orientation to the future. They are often interested in the abstract and in theory, and may enjoy activities where they can use symbols or be creative. Their memory of things is often an impression of what they thought was the essence of an event, rather than a memory of the literal words or experiences associated with the event. They often like concepts in and of themselves, even ones that do not have an immediate application, and they learn best when they have an impression of the overall idea first.

People who prefer intuition may:
▪ recall events by what they read "between the lines" at the time
▪ solve problems through quick insight and through making leaps
▪ be interested in doing things that are new and different
▪ work from the big picture to the facts
▪ place great trust in insights, symbols, and metaphors and less in what is literally experienced
▪ *sometimes* focus so much on new possibilities that they miss the practicalities of bringing them into reality

Thinking and Feeling

This third preference pair describes how you like to make decisions or come to closure about the information you have taken in using your sensing or intuition. In other words, what kind of *judgment* do you prefer to use? A person of good judgment is able make distinctions among a variety of choices and settle on a course of action that demonstrates excellence of understanding. You can make these rational ordered judgments in two ways: by giving more weight to objective principles and the impersonal facts (thinking), or to personal and human concerns, and the people issues (feeling).

Thinking (T)	Feeling (F)
Key words:	Key words:
impersonal ■ truth ■ cool ■ tough-minded	**personal ■ value ■ warm ■ tender-hearted**
People who have a preference for thinking judgment are concerned with determining the objective truth in a situation. More impersonal in approach, thinking types believe they can make the best decisions by removing personal concerns that may lead to biased analyses and decision making. Thinking types seek to act based on the truth in a situation, a truth or principle that is independent of what they or others might want to believe or wish were true. The thinking function is concerned with logical consistency and analysis of cause and effect. As they use and develop their thinking function, thinking types often come to appear analytical, cool, and tough-minded.	People who have a preference for feeling judgment are concerned with whether decisions and actions are worthwhile. More personal in approach, feeling types believe they can make the best decisions by weighing what people care about and the points-of-view of persons involved in a situation. Feeling types are concerned with personal values and with making decisions based on a ranking of greater to lesser importance— what is the *best* for the people involved. The feeling function places high value on relatedness between people, and feeling types are often concerned with establishing or maintaining harmony in their relationships. As they use and develop their feeling function, feeling types often come to appear caring, warm, and tactful. Remember, in type language, feeling does not mean being "emotional;" rather, it is a way of reasoning.
People who prefer thinking may: ■ have a technical or scientific orientation ■ be concerned with truth and notice inconsistencies ■ look for logical explanations or solutions to most everything ■ make decisions with their heads and want to be fair ■ believe telling the whole truth is more important than being tactful ■ *sometimes* miss seeing or valuing the "people" part of situations and be experienced by others as too task-oriented, uncaring, or indifferent	People who prefer feeling may: ■ have a people or communications orientation ■ be concerned with harmony and be aware when it is missing ■ look for what is important to others and express concern for others ■ make decisions with their hearts and want to be compassionate ■ believe being tactful is more important than telling the "cold" truth ■ *sometimes* miss seeing or communicating about the "hard truth" of situations and be experienced by others as too idealistic, mushy, or indirect

Judging and Perceiving

This fourth preference pair describes how you like to live your outer life—what are the behaviors that others tend to see? Do you prefer a more structured and decided lifestyle (judging) or a more flexible and adaptable lifestyle (perceiving)? This preference may also be thought of as your *orientation to the outer world*.

Another way of saying this is that the judging-perceiving preference describes the nature of our extraversion—because we all extravert at times, even introverts, and all extraverts introvert at times. This scale asks us when we extravert, do we extravert a judging (J) function (our favorite of thinking or feeling), or do we extravert a perceiving (P) function (our favorite of sensing or intuition)? There is more about this issue in the section *The Dynamic Basis for Type.*

Everyone uses judgment and perception all of the time. In fact, that is the basis for type. You need both perception and judgment. However, when it comes to dealing with the outer world, people tend to stay more in either the structured/decided mode or in the flexible/adaptable mode.

Judging (J)

Key words:

**structured ■ decided
   organized ■ scheduled**

People who have a preference for judging use their preferred judging function (whether it is thinking or feeling) in their outer life. What this often looks like is that they prefer a planned or orderly way of life, like to have things settled and organized, feel more comfortable when decisions are made, and like to bring life under control to the degree that it is possible. Since they are using either their T or F in their outer world, they want to make decisions to bring things in their outer life to closure. Remember though, this only describes how their outer life looks. Inside, they may feel flexible and open to new information (which they are). Remember, in type language, judging means "preferring to make decisions;" it does not mean "judgmental" in the sense of constantly making negative evaluations about people and events.

People who prefer judging may:
■ like to make decisions, or at least like to have things decided
■ look task oriented
■ like to make lists of things to do
■ like to get their work done before playing
■ plan work to avoid rushing just before deadline
■ *sometimes* make decisions too quickly without enough information
■ *sometimes* focus so much on the goal or plan that they miss the need to change directions at times

Perceiving (P)

Key words:

**flexible ■ open
   adaptable ■ spontaneous**

People who have a preference for perceiving use their preferred perceiving function (whether it is sensing or intuition) in their outer life. What this often looks like is that they prefer a more flexible and spontaneous way of life, like to understand and adapt to the world, and like to stay open to new experiences. Since they are using either their S or N in their outer world, they want to continue to take in new information. Remember again that this only describes how the person's outer life looks. Inside they may feel very planful or decisive (which they are). Remember, in type language perceiving means "preferring to take in information;" it does not mean "perceptive" in the sense of having quick and accurate perceptions about people and events.

People who prefer perceiving may:
■ like staying open to respond to whatever happens
■ look more loose and casual
■ like to keep laid-out plans to a minimum
■ like to approach work as play or mix work and play
■ work in bursts of energy, and enjoy rushing just before deadlines
■ *sometimes* stay open to new information so long that they miss making decisions
■ *sometimes* focus so much on adapting to the moment that they do not settle on a direction or plan

Your Type Is the Combination of Your Preferences on the Four Scales

The preferences you expressed on each of the four scales combine to yield a four-letter type pattern which is your *psychological type*. For example, preferences for introversion (I), sensing (S), thinking (T), and judging (J) combine to yield the four-letter type pattern ISTJ. These four preferences interact in dynamic and complex ways that can tell you much about who you are and how you approach the world. There are sixteen different combinations of the preferences (e.g., INFP, ESFJ, ENTP), and descriptions of these sixteen types begin on page 14.

Before you read the descriptions, you may find it useful to read the following sections. If you have already taken the MBTI, the next section *What Do My Scores Mean?* will help you interpret your results.

The section *The Dynamic Basis for Type* explains just how the type preferences interact to yield the pattern of personality we call "type." That section also describes how your type can show up in your lifelong development, and how your environment can affect the development of your type. Those having difficulty clarifying their preferences may find that section especially helpful.

What Do My Scores Mean?
(For those who have taken the MBTI)

When you took the MBTI, your results appeared on a report form as numbers and/or dark lines representing the clarity of your preferences on each of the scales (EI, SN, TF, JP). The Indicator was designed to point in the direction of your preference and nothing more. Preference scores come from comparing the votes you cast for each preference as you responded to each question. The more you voted in one direction the higher the score, and the more you split your vote the lower the score. The scores are a by-product of determining the *direction* of preference. Thus, scores should only be interpreted as a measure of how confident we are that you were able to see your preferences clearly in the questions.

Research shows that as your preference score gets larger, we can have increasing confidence that your true preferences were reported on the Indicator. Research does *not* show that having a higher score means you are better at the skills of your preference than someone with lower scores. The Indicator does not ask us to report on the quality with which we use our preferences. It only asks us to vote between different but equally valuable choices.

If your scores are very close to the middle on one or more scales, then you should read your type description with more caution to be sure it fits. A low score usually means you split your vote. This may mean that either the Indicator does not have the right questions to help you identify your preferences, or that you see yourself using a mixture of behaviors from both sides of the preference pair. Either way, you will probably need to spend some time exploring what your true preferences might be. You can do so through observing yourself more closely, from talking with your MBTI practitioner or people who know you, and from reading more lengthy type descriptions.

People report behaviors that come from different sides of a preference pair for many reasons. The most basic reason is that everybody learns skills from both sides of the preference pair, and people try to draw on the skills that are needed for a given situation. As a result, you may have answered questions on the MBTI describing how you behave in a particular situation, but the behavior described is markedly different from your general style. For example, you may have to be structured (J) in your job, but spontaneity (P) is more your natural style. In this case, your preference scores on J or P could be lower.

Low scores, however, are not wrong. We just have less confidence that they represent your true preferences. You simply need to be careful accepting the results as true until you have further explored how your preferences might be expressing themselves. Remember, it is your *preference* for one or the other side of the scale that is important, *not* the size of the score. Do not overinterpret the scores.

The Dynamic Basis for Type

In this section, you will get a glimpse of how your type is more than just the combination of your four letters; it is in fact a dynamic and complex interrelated system of personality. You will learn how the different parts of your type work with each other to make you a balanced and effective person, how your type develops throughout life, and how people can sometimes get pushed off their natural path of development.

The Mental Functions

In type language, you have four mental functions: sensing, intuition, thinking, and feeling. Remember that extraversion and introversion are *attitudes*, and judging and perceiving are *orientations to the outer world*. The four mental functions are the basis for much of your mental activity.

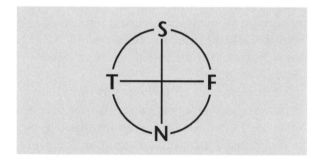

Two are for gathering information—that is, they are used for perceiving:

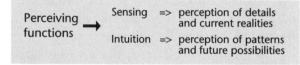

Two are for organizing information and for making decisions—that is, they are used for judging:

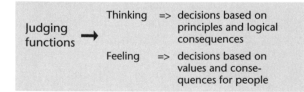

Knowing how the four functions relate to each other, and in what order you prefer them, can tell you a great deal about yourself: how you prefer to communicate, what you consider to be important, the kinds of activities and careers you find motivating or stressful, and many other things.

Everyone Uses All Four Mental Functions, But People Prefer Them in a Certain Order

Everyone has and uses sensing, intuition, thinking, and feeling; in fact, you couldn't get through the day without using all four to some degree! People just differ in the order in which they prefer to use them and the order in which they develop them as they grow. For example, for some people logical closure (T) is the most important thing, then secondarily they attend to the facts and details (S). They give less weight to the possibilities (N), and the least weight to the people-impact of decisions (F). For someone else the order might be just the reverse, or some other order entirely.

In type theory, the order in which we prefer these processes is inborn. *The four-letter type formula is a shorthand way of telling us about the order in which a person prefers to use the four mental functions.*

Table One summarizes the order in which each type prefers the mental functions.

The Dominant Function: Everyone has one favorite function among the four functions, and everyone uses that favorite function in their favorite (Extraverted or Introverted) world.

We develop one of these four mental functions to a greater degree than any of the other three. This first and favorite function is like the captain of a ship, having the most important role in guiding us, and it becomes the type core of our conscious personality. This mental function is called the *dominant* function. During the first part of your life, you come to rely on your favorite function, and you tend to develop the most skills with it.

Some people, for example, give the most weight to their intuition. They trust that function the most and they are the most energized when they use it. As children, they probably tended to focus on intuition (assuming their family supported it), and they probably became involved in activities where they could use their imagination and focus on possibilities.

Extraverts by definition prefer to live in the outer world. Therefore they use their dominant function in the outer world. They put their best foot forward. Thus, dominant intuitives who are extraverts turn their intuition to the outer world. You are likely to see their intuition in their outward behavior when you meet them. They would likely be actively involved in an ongoing stream of new ideas, projects, and activities.

Introverts by definition prefer to live in their inner world. Therefore they use their dominant function in their inner world. Thus, dominant intuitives who are introverts turn their intuition to their inner world. They would most likely be interested in reflecting on new ideas and on new ways images, concepts, and symbols fit together. You are likely to see their intuition only after getting to know them, and if they tell you what is going on in their inner world.

You will likely want to trust your dominant function in your life and be sure you have plenty of opportunities to use it, though you will still need to use your other functions as well. The dominant function is one of the two middle letters of your four-letter type pattern. Look at Table One to see which is your dominant function and how it is oriented.

Table One: Priorities of Functions

ISTJ	ISFJ	INFJ	INTJ
1) Sensing (Dominant) – I	1) Sensing (Dominant) – I	1) Intuition (Dominant) – I	1) Intuition (Dominant) – I
2) Thinking (Auxiliary) – E	2) Feeling (Auxiliary) – E	2) Feeling (Auxiliary) – E	2) Thinking (Auxiliary) – E
3) Feeling (Tertiary) – E/I	3) Thinking (Tertiary) – E/I	3) Thinking (Tertiary) – E/I	3) Feeling (Tertiary) – E/I
4) Intuition (Inferior) – E	4) Intuition (Inferior) – E	4) Sensing (Inferior) – E	4) Sensing (Inferior) – E

ISTP	ISFP	INFP	INTP
1) Thinking (Dominant) – I	1) Feeling (Dominant) – I	1) Feeling (Dominant) – I	1) Thinking (Dominant) – I
2) Sensing (Auxiliary) – E	2) Sensing (Auxiliary) – E	2) Intuition (Auxiliary) – E	2) Intuition (Auxiliary) – E
3) Intuition (Tertiary) – E/I	3) Intuition (Tertiary) – E/I	3) Sensing (Tertiary) – E/I	3) Sensing (Tertiary) – E/I
4) Feeling (Inferior) – E	4) Thinking (Inferior) – E	4) Thinking (Inferior) – E	4) Feeling (Inferior) – E

ESTP	ESFP	ENFP	ENTP
1) Sensing (Dominant) – E	1) Sensing (Dominant) – E	1) Intuition (Dominant) – E	1) Intuition (Dominant) – E
2) Thinking (Auxiliary) – I	2) Feeling (Auxiliary) – I	2) Feeling (Auxiliary) – I	2) Thinking (Auxiliary) – I
3) Feeling (Tertiary) – E/I	3) Thinking (Tertiary) – E/I	3) Thinking (Tertiary) – E/I	3) Feeling (Tertiary) – E/I
4) Intuition (Inferior) – I	4) Intuition (Inferior) – I	4) Sensing (Inferior) – I	4) Sensing (Inferior) – I

ESTJ	ESFJ	ENFJ	ENTJ
1) Thinking (Dominant) – E	1) Feeling (Dominant) – E	1) Feeling (Dominant) – E	1) Thinking (Dominant) – E
2) Sensing (Auxiliary) – I	2) Sensing (Auxiliary) – I	2) Intuition (Auxiliary) – I	2) Intuition (Auxiliary) – I
3) Intuition (Tertiary) – E/I	3) Intuition (Tertiary) – E/I	3) Sensing (Tertiary) – E/I	3) Sensing (Tertiary) – E/I
4) Feeling (Inferior) – I	4) Thinking (Inferior) – I	4) Thinking (Inferior) – I	4) Feeling (Inferior) – I

E = Extraverted   I = Introverted   E/I = Theorists differ on the orientation of the tertiary.

The Auxiliary Function: Everyone has a second favorite function that gives balance to their dominant function.

If individuals used only the dominant function all of the time, then they would be too one-sided. The second favorite function is called the *auxiliary*, because it helps give *balance* to the dominant function. The auxiliary function is very important in your life but always ranks second in importance to your dominant function. Your auxiliary function is the other of the two middle letters of your four-letter type pattern.

There are two ways your auxiliary gives balance to your dominant function.

1) The auxiliary helps you balance judging and perceiving. For good type development, everyone needs to be reasonably comfortable and skillful with a judging function (T or F) and with a perceiving function (S or N). *Everyone* needs to be able to take in new information, and *everyone* needs to be able to come to closure or make decisions about that information. The auxiliary helps ensure you do both.

If a person were all perception, he or she would be blown around like a small boat with an oversized sail and a small keel—driven by any and every change in wind direction.* Such a person would be constantly drawn by new perceptions (whether sensing or intuition) but have difficulty making decisions or coming to conclusions. In contrast, if a person were all judgment, he or she would be like a boat with a very large keel and a small sail—very sure and stable, but not open to new input from the wind. Such a person would be sure of his or her decisions (whether using thinking or feeling), but would not be able to take in new and needed information to modify his or her behavior as conditions changed.

If someone's dominant function is a perceiving function (S or N), a well-developed auxiliary function (T or F) helps that individual make judgments (decisions). The reverse is also true. If someone's dominant function is a judging function, a well-developed auxiliary function helps that individual stay open to new perceptions.

Figure One: The auxiliary balances judging and perceiving

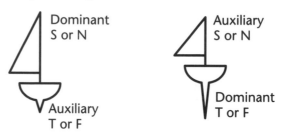

Dominant S or N / Auxiliary T or F

Auxiliary S or N / Dominant T or F

Dominant intuitives, for example, have thinking or feeling as their auxiliary function. If they prefer feeling, then we would typically find that the feeling function developed next in their life after intuition. They would still give the most weight to their intuitive perceptions, but then they would make use of their feeling to reason and to make decisions about those intuitive perceptions.

2) The auxiliary helps you balance extraversion and introversion. *Everyone* needs to be able to pay attention to the outer world and to move into action, and *everyone* needs to be able to pause for reflection and to pay attention to their inner world. Extraverts need to be able to turn to their inner world at times, and introverts need to be able to turn to the outer world at times. The auxiliary function helps in this balancing act.

As you saw before, if you are an extravert, you use your dominant function in the outside world. For balance, you use your auxiliary function in the inner world. The outer world is of more importance to you, but your auxiliary is what you use to be involved in your inner world. Without using their auxiliary, extraverts would never stop to reflect.

If you are an introvert, you use your dominant function in your inner world. For balance, you use your auxiliary function in the outer world. The inner world is of more interest to you, but your auxiliary is what you use to be involved in the outer world. Without using their auxiliary, introverts would never move into action.

*Gordon Lawrence first described the judging-perceiving balance in this way.

Thus, dominant extraverted intuitives who prefer feeling use their feeling function in their inner world. You are more likely to see their intuition than their feeling when you first meet them. Dominant introverted intuitives who prefer feeling use their feeling function in the outer world. You are more likely to encounter their feeling when you first meet them.

Figure Two: The auxiliary balances extraversion and introversion.

Dominant extraverted intuition
Auxiliary introverted feeling

Dominant introverted intuition
Auxiliary extraverted feeling

F)N   N)F

Now you can see why it's so important to have good development of both your auxiliary and your dominant functions. Look at Table One to see which is your auxiliary function and which way you direct it.

The Tertiary and Inferior Functions: Your third and fourth-preferred functions tend to be less interesting to you, and you tend to have fewer skills associated with them.

Your third-preferred function is called your *tertiary,* and your fourth-preferred function is called your *least-preferred* or *inferior* function. These functions do not show up directly in your four-letter type formula, but you can see what they are for your type by looking at Table One.

Though you use all four mental functions, your third and fourth-preferred functions tend to be less interesting and less well-developed than your dominant and auxiliary functions. You tend to use them less consciously. As you grow and develop, you learn that there is a time and place to use your third and fourth functions as well. Your development of these functions tends to occur later in your life, and you may experience great satisfaction in their development. However, because you have given less conscious attention to developing them, they always tend to lag behind your dominant and auxiliary in skill level.

For example, if intuition and feeling are your two most favored functions, then you will probably be more inclined to focus on the future, the abstract, harmony, and especially "possibilities for people." You might also have some difficulty developing interests or skills in using your sensing and thinking, because these are the opposites of your natural preferences. For example, you would probably have less interest in developing skills in the impersonal analysis of technical data.

Your inferior, or least well developed function, is the opposite (i.e., the other preference in the preference pair) from your dominant function. This function generally provides you with clues about which areas of your life you tend to avoid and involves skills you tend to have the hardest time developing. For example, if thinking were your dominant function, feeling would be your least-preferred function. You would probably have significantly less interest in and fewer skills with the feeling function (e.g., attending to harmony in relationships, giving weight to the personal aspects of decision making).

Extended use of your inferior function, and your tertiary to some degree, tends to require a great deal of energy, and ongoing use of them may leave you feeling stressed or tired.

Lifelong Development

It is not a hard and fast rule, but people generally tend to develop the four functions throughout their lives in the order in which they prefer them (see Table One). As you grow and move through life, the way you see the world and how you behave tends to change and broaden. Thus you may be very different at midlife than you were in high school. This is due not only to your gaining experience but also to your development of the four functions. As you spend time later in life developing your tertiary and least-preferred functions, the range of behaviors available to you and the career and lifestyle options you consider may open up.

Remember, even as you use and develop your tertiary and inferior functions, your dominant and auxiliary functions will always be your favorites. Build on their strengths earlier in your life because they are the core functions of your conscious personality and the basis for much of your self-esteem.

Discovering Your True Type and Type Falsification

As we have said, people tend to develop the functions in the order in which they prefer them. If family, school, and environment support this natural path, individuals will come to use and trust most their dominant function, followed by increasing use and trust of their auxiliary function. Your true type is the type that represents your *natural* preferences.

Sometimes family, school, and culture do not allow individuals to develop along their natural paths. For example, a child who tries to make logical and objective decisions using thinking may be made to feel guilty for not attending enough to family harmony and other feeling values. In this manner, an individual *may* be discouraged from developing his or her naturally preferred dominant and/or auxiliary functions, and instead be pushed to develop another less-preferred function first. This kind of type *falsification* may lead to a person's not feeling comfortable with his or her ability to make good decisions or not knowing what is important information to attend to in his or her life. For these and other reasons, a person may feel tension between some preferences (between thinking and feeling, or between sensing and intuition) and not be sure which is his or her natural preference.

When you read your type description, and it seems mostly on target for you, start with the assumption that this is your true type. If your type description does not fit you well or if you have questions about it, listen to yourself and try reading some other descriptions. For example, if it is clear to you that you have preferences for E, F, and J but you are not sure if you prefer S or N, try reading both descriptions: ESFJ and ENFJ. Most often one will fit you much better than the other. If you are still having difficulty determining your preferences, you may find it helpful to read other descriptions or to talk with someone who knows type well, and who may be able to help you clarify your true type.

Everyone is different, and you may not have a clear preference on one or more scales at this time. That's fine. Take as much time as you need to explore the different descriptions of the preferences and of the sixteen types. Since everyone is an individual, the entire type description may not fit you; this is because there is much more to people than type, and because everyone has a different life history. Discovering your true type is part of the larger life-long process of getting to know who you are: a worthwhile endeavor. Remember, since you are the expert on you, you are the one who ultimately decides which type description fits you best, and which type is your true type.

The Sixteen Type Descriptions

Now that you know more about the dynamic interactions of the functions for the types, you will be able to see how the type descriptions in the next section are organized by dynamics. In fact, the title of each type description tells you what the dominant and auxiliary functions are for that type (e.g., ESTJ—Extraverted Thinking with Introverted Sensing). As you read about the types, you may notice that the description starts out with an emphasis on the dominant function and how it is the essence of someone's type. The description then moves on to how the auxiliary adds to that type's behavioral style and how the preferences all combine to influence the needs, interests, and relationships of someone with that type. Finally, the description addresses what may happen if the auxiliary is not developed, and how the least-preferred function may show up in that type's life.

The Sixteen Types at a Glance

ISTJ

For ISTJs the dominant quality in their lives is an abiding sense of responsibility for doing what needs to be done in the here-and-now. Their realism, organizing abilities, and command of the facts lead to their completing tasks thoroughly and with great attention to detail. Logical pragmatists at heart, ISTJs make decisions based on their experience and with an eye to efficiency in all things. ISTJs are intensely committed to people and to the organizations of which they are a part; they take their work seriously and believe others should do so as well.

ISFJ

For ISFJs the dominant quality in their lives is an abiding respect and sense of personal responsibility for doing what needs to be done in the here-and-now. Actions that are of practical help to others are of particular importance to ISFJs. Their realism, organizing abilities, and command of the facts lead to their thorough attention in completing tasks. ISFJs bring an aura of quiet warmth, caring, and dependability to all that they do; they take their work seriously and believe others should do so as well.

ISTP

For ISTPs the driving force in their lives is to understand how things and phenomena in the real world work so they can make the best and most effective use of them. They are logical and realistic people, and they are natural trouble-shooters. When not actively solving a problem, ISTPs are quiet and analytical observers of their environment, and they naturally look for the underlying sense to any facts they have gathered. ISTPs often pursue variety and even excitement in their hands-on experiences. Although they do have a spontaneous, even playful side, what people often first encounter with them is their detached pragmatism.

ISFP

For ISFPs the dominant quality in their lives is a deep-felt caring for living things, combined with a quietly playful and sometimes adventurous approach to life and all its experiences. ISFPs typically show their caring in very practical ways, since they often prefer action to words. Their warmth and concern are generally not expressed openly, and what people often first encounter with ISFPs is their quiet adaptability, realism, and "free spirit" spontaneity.

ESTP

For ESTPs the dominant quality in their lives is their enthusiastic attention to the outer world of hands-on and real-life experiences. ESTPs are excited by continuous involvement in new activities and in the pursuit of new challenges. They tend to be logical and analytical in their approach to life, and they have an acute sense of how objects, events, and people in the world work. ESTPs are typically energetic and adaptable realists, who prefer to experience and accept life rather than to judge or organize it.

ESFP

For ESFPs the dominant quality in their lives is their enthusiastic attention to the outer world of hands-on and real-life experiences. ESFPs are excited by continuous involvement in new activities and new relationships. They also have a deep concern for people, and they show their caring in warm and pragmatic gestures of helping. ESFPs are typically energetic and adaptable realists, who prefer to experience and accept life rather than to judge or organize it.

ESTJ

For ESTJs the driving force in their lives is their need to analyze and bring into logical order the outer world of events, people, and things. ESTJs like to organize anything that comes into their domain, and they will work energetically to complete tasks so they can quickly move from one to the next. Sensing orients their thinking to current facts and realities, and thus gives their thinking a pragmatic quality. ESTJs take their responsibilities seriously and believe others should do so as well.

ESFJ

For ESFJs the dominant quality in their lives is an active and intense caring about people and a strong desire to bring harmony into their relationships. ESFJs bring an aura of warmth to all that they do, and they naturally move into action to help others, to organize the world around them, and to get things done. Sensing orients their feeling to current facts and realities, and thus gives their feeling a hands-on pragmatic quality. ESFJs take their work seriously and believe others should do so as well.

INFJ

For INFJs the dominant quality in their lives is their attention to the inner world of possibilities, ideas, and symbols. Knowing by way of insight is paramount for them, and they often manifest a deep concern for people and relationships as well. INFJs often have deep interests in creative expression as well as issues of spirituality and human development. While their energy and attention are naturally drawn to the inner world of ideas and insights, what people often first encounter with INFJs is their drive for closure and for the application of their ideas to people's concerns.

INFP

For INFPs the dominant quality in their lives is a deep-felt caring and idealism about people. They experience this intense caring most often in their relationships with others, but they may also experience it around ideas, projects, or any involvement they see as important. INFPs are often skilled communicators, and they are naturally drawn to ideas that embody a concern for human potential. INFPs live in the inner world of values and ideals, but what people often first encounter with them in the outer world is their adaptability and concern for possibilities.

ENFP

For ENFPs the dominant quality in their lives is their attention to the outer world of possibilities; they are excited by continuous involvement in anything new, whether it be new ideas, new people, or new activities. Though ENFPs thrive on what is possible and what is new, they also experience a deep concern for people as well. Thus, they are especially interested in possibilities for people. ENFPs are typically energetic, enthusiastic people who lead spontaneous and adaptable lives.

ENFJ

For ENFJs the dominant quality in their lives is an active and intense caring about people and a strong desire to bring harmony into their relationships. ENFJs are openly expressive and empathic people who bring an aura of warmth to all that they do. Intuition orients their feeling to the new and to the possible, thus they often enjoy working to manifest a humanitarian vision, or helping others develop their potential. ENFJs naturally and conscientiously move into action to care for others, to organize the world around them, and to get things done.

INTJ

For INTJs the dominant force in their lives is their attention to the inner world of possibilities, symbols, abstractions, images, and thoughts. Insight in conjunction with logical analysis is the essence of their approach to the world; they think systemically. Ideas are the substance of life for INTJs and they have a driving need to understand, to know, and to demonstrate competence in their areas of interest. INTJs inherently trust their insights, and with their task-orientation will work intensely to make their visions into realities.

INTP

For INTPs the driving force in their lives is to understand whatever phenomenon is the focus of their attention. They want to make sense of the world—as a concept—and they often enjoy opportunities to be creative. INTPs are logical, analytical, and detached in their approach to the world; they naturally question and critique ideas and events as they strive for understanding. INTPs usually have little need to control the outer world, or to bring order to it, and they often appear very flexible and adaptable in their lifestyle.

ENTP

For ENTPs the dominant quality in their lives is their attention to the outer world of possibilities; they are excited by continuous involvement in anything new, whether it be new ideas, new people, or new activities. They look for patterns and meaning in the world, and they often have a deep need to analyze, to understand, and to know the nature of things. ENTPs are typically energetic, enthusiastic people who lead spontaneous and adaptable lives.

ENTJ

For ENTJs the driving force in their lives is their need to analyze and bring into logical order the outer world of events, people, and things. ENTJs are natural leaders who build conceptual models that serve as plans for strategic action. Intuition orients their thinking to the future, and gives their thinking an abstract quality. ENTJs will actively pursue and direct others in the pursuit of goals they have set, and they prefer a world that is structured and organized.

Descriptions of the Sixteen Types

ISTJ
Introverted Sensing with Extraverted Thinking

For ISTJs the dominant quality in their lives is an abiding sense of responsibility for doing what needs to be done in the here-and-now. Their realism, organizing abilities, and command of the facts lead to their completing tasks thoroughly and with great attention to detail. Logical pragmatists at heart, ISTJs make decisions based on their experience and with an eye to efficiency in all things. ISTJs are intensely committed to people and to the organizations of which they are a part; they take their work seriously and believe others should do so as well.

ISTJs are quiet, serious, and realistic observers of their environment, who naturally attend to and remember concrete facts. They give great weight to hands-on life experiences; they use their sensing to internally process and file away data for later use. ISTJs usually have a massive amount of information stored inside and an impressive command of the facts. In recalling a past event, they often have a good memory for what was literally said or done. Their orientation to detail can also show as a concern for precision in action and in speech. It was an ISTJ who originally said, "Say what you mean."

ISTJs bring a detached pragmatism to all that they do, and they have a great deal of common sense; ISTJs are typically down-to-earth folk. They learn by doing, and want to know how an idea can be used or applied. As a result, they are often quite skeptical people. "Seeing is believing." They respect the facts and their experience, and they expect things to be logical. Period.

Thinking gives order and structure to ISTJs' experiences and puts their pragmatism in a logical context. ISTJs tend to be analytical and tough-minded, and they make decisions with an eye to impersonal consequences; they really want their decisions to be objective and fair. Thinking in conjunction with sensing also gives them an eye to the efficient manipulation of real-world phenomena. That is, they like to bring logical order to facts and things in their environment. ISTJs are usually more oriented to the tasks on which they are working than to the people with whom they work, and they may sometimes unrealistically expect all people to behave "logically."

ISTJs do like a structured and organized outer world, and find comfort in developing and adhering to a routine in their work. They like to know what their job is, and generally do not appreciate settings where the rules constantly change; in this sense, ISTJs are conservative. They guard what works, and they want to see evidence that a new way will work before they adopt it. "If it works, why change it?" This attitude gives them an atmosphere of patience and stability, and others often feel settled and calm in their presence.

Above all else, ISTJs are responsible. They do things just because they need to be done, and they have a powerful work ethic. "Work hard, *then* play." ISTJs like getting things done, and they are thorough as they carry a task through to completion. Once an ISTJ commits to complete a task, he or she will do so; they are exceptionally dependable. In fact, they can be difficult to distract once they have begun to systematically work on a project. "Plan your work, and work your plan." ISTJs honor their commitments, and they expect others to do the same; they hold themselves and others accountable for getting things done.

Tradition, stability, and preparedness are usually valued by ISTJs. They respect the fine-tuned performance that characterizes established organizations, and they are often found working in such settings. Through their conscientiousness as well as by quietly building community, ISTJs form much of the backbone of society. They also provide stability through their often clear sense of what constitutes appropriate and inappropriate behavior, and through the keeping of traditions. Ceremonies and anniversaries, such as weddings, birthdays, and holidays, are valued and celebrated.

With their memory for facts and with their attention to getting things done, ISTJs often have great academic success, particularly in subjects that have applications and where results can be seen. Though they tend to have less interest in highly theoretical subjects, they can certainly succeed there as well.

ISTJs are often found in business, production, banking, law, auditing, engineering, and other areas where a mastery of factual data and a tough-minded concern for organization is needed. In their domain, ISTJs work toward efficiency and conservation of resources; they are naturals for quality control. They are often found in management or supervisory positions, overseeing the practical realization of institutional goals. Though they often like to work alone, ISTJs are willing and able to delegate work to ensure the business of the day gets done.

In relationships ISTJs look for fair play and dependability. They themselves tend to be quiet and serious; they are people of few words. They are inclined to be straightforward in their communications and controlled in the outward expression of their emotions. ISTJs do often have a hidden but quirky sense of humor that arises from their highly individual reactions to events. In the extreme, ISTJs may be insensitive and miss the "people part of the equation." At times, they may appear intolerant, and at worst, they may run over others who do not communicate their asser-

tions in a logical and succinct manner.

Development of their extraverted thinking will help ISTJs become more action-oriented and effective in the outer world. Otherwise, they may end up immersed and trapped in their inner world of impressions and memories. Development of thinking will help bring order to their lives by helping them decide which are the most appropriate actions for them to take, and development of flexibility will help them avoid becoming too focused on details. ISTJs may need to work especially hard to understand others' needs for appreciation and emotional support; after all, they are inclined to overlook even their own contributions. Development of feeling will ultimately help them attend more to the people impact of their words and actions. Further, development of intuition will give them a greater respect for the big picture consequences of some of their actions and a greater appreciation for theory.

Under stress ISTJs may withdraw, focus only on their work, and burn out through pushing themselves to get too many things done. They may also become rigid about following rules and become excessively critical of others. Under extreme stress, they can become intensely pessimistic, seeing only negative possibilities in the future, for themselves, for others, and for the world at large.

Key words

detail ■ precision ■ duty

conscientious ■ analytical ■ critique ■ cool ■ responsibility

ISFJ
Introverted Sensing with
Extraverted Feeling

For ISFJs the dominant quality in their lives is an abiding respect and sense of personal responsibility for doing what needs to be done in the here-and-now. Actions that are of practical help to others are of particular importance to ISFJs. Their realism, organizing abilities, and command of the facts lead to their thorough attention in completing tasks. ISFJs bring an aura of quiet warmth, caring, and dependability to all that they do; they take their work seriously and believe others should do so as well.

ISFJs are quiet and realistic observers of their environment. They naturally attend to, and have a good memory for, concrete details. ISFJs trust their experience. As they gain hands-on life experiences, they use their sensing to process and file away data for later use. ISFJs usually have a massive amount of data stored inside and an impressive command of the facts. In recalling a past conversation or event, they often have a good memory for what was literally said or done. They like people to be precise in their communications, just as they themselves are.

ISFJs tend to be concrete and pragmatic people. They learn by doing, and they feel that "seeing is believing." They have less interest in abstractions and are more interested in what can be used or applied. ISFJs are down-to-earth in their approach to life, and they tend to have a lot of common sense.

Feeling gives order and structure to ISFJs' experience and puts their pragmatism in a people context. They make decisions based on people values and with attention to human consequences, while sensing ensures that they base their decisions on personal experience. Harmony in relationships is a core value for ISFJs. Feeling also gives them a clear sense of right and wrong and a deep concern for the common welfare. They want their actions to be of benefit to others, and they often quietly radiate compassion. ISFJs at the very least prefer that their actions cause no harm. Though they can be uncomfortable confronting others, they will do so if they believe someone they care about may be harmed.

Above all else, ISFJs take responsibility very seriously and very personally; they have a powerful work ethic. "Work hard, *then* play." ISFJs work persistently and thoroughly, and they hold themselves accountable to get things done. When they promise someone they will do something, they will do it. Because they are so conscientious, ISFJs can be difficult to distract from a task to which they have committed themselves.

Organizational structure, continuity, and security are usually valued by the ISFJs. They want to know the expectations associated with their job and with the jobs of others. If ISFJs can find a cause for which to work, so much the better, because their loyalty will make them tireless supporters of the mission. Through quietly building community, they form much of the backbone of society. In their concern for stability, ISFJs may find themselves acting as guardians of history and tradition. Holidays, anniversaries, and ceremonies are observed, and memories, particularly those of people and relationships, are held in fond regard. Needless to say, family relationships are deep and enduring connections for ISFJs.

ISFJs like to preserve what works. "If it works, why change it?" This attitude gives ISFJs an atmosphere of stability, and others will often feel settled and calm in their presence. Since they often enjoy developing and adhering to a routine in their work, settings where the rules constantly change can be frustrating to them. Though they tend to be conservative, ISFJs are willing to change if there is good evidence of the need. However, they are always concerned that the results be practical and workable.

ISFJs can be frustrated by too much theory and abstraction, and by too much logical analysis; the hard theoretical sciences are often a turnoff. They do, however, learn well in classrooms that give weight to orderly, planful study, and which demonstrate applications of what is learned. ISFJs can master an amazing number of facts.

ISFJs typically like opportunities to interact with people, and they are often found in careers where they can nurture others or attend to their pragmatic physical, emotional, and spiritual needs. They are usually good listeners, and they may have a special affinity with children. ISFJs are often found in health care, religious careers, and teaching (particularly K-12). They are found in business as well, where their pragmatism, organization, and attention to the needs of the customer can lead to great success. Their willingness to take on responsibility can lead to their being placed in management roles, in which positions they are very attentive to the needs of people. They may, however, struggle to learn to delegate tasks.

In their relationships, ISFJs are sympathetic and considerate, and they like to feel a sense of belonging. They tend to be people of few words—quiet but warm. Do not be misled, however, because intimate relationships are of extreme importance to ISFJs. They are deeply loyal to the people about whom they care. They usually make good team members and need to be appreciated for their contributions, though they tend to be modest about their own accomplishments. ISFJs may also have a hidden but quirky sense of humor that arises from their highly individual reactions to events. They may be very sensitive to criticism or lack of appreciation and are in danger of bottling up their emotions and resentments.

Development of their extraverted feeling will help ISFJs become more action-oriented and effective in the outer world. Otherwise, they may end up immersed in their inner world of impressions and trapped in negative reactions. Development of feeling will help bring order to their lives by helping them decide what is most important for them to pursue. In their desire for harmony, ISFJs' own needs may not get expressed or met, and they may respond too much to what others feel or believe. They could benefit from taking the initiative and from being more assertive. Development of intuition and thinking will help them not only to properly estimate their contributions but also to see more of the long-range consequences of their actions, and to be open to new ways of doing things.

Under stress, ISFJs can become rigid, blindly following rules and regulations. If they are not appreciated they may withdraw and/or complain in nonconstructive ways. Under great stress, they may feel deep fatigue and internalize all of their tensions. In the extreme, ISFJs can become exceptionally pessimistic, and see only negative possibilities as they look forward to a fearful future.

Key words

quiet warmth ■ responsible ■ dependable
conscientious ■ systematic ■ realistic ■ pragmatic helper

INFJ
Introverted Intuition with Extraverted Feeling

For INFJs the dominant quality in their lives is their attention to the inner world of possibilities, ideas, and symbols. Knowing by way of insight is paramount for them, and they often manifest a deep concern for people and relationships as well. INFJs often have deep interests in creative expression as well as issues of spirituality and human development. While their energy and attention are naturally drawn to the inner world of ideas and insights, what people often first encounter with INFJs is their drive for closure and for the application of their ideas to people's concerns.

Ideas and symbols are real for INFJs. They live for insight and imagination, and they move freely in the inner world of ideas. Their reasoning is abstract, conceptual, complex, and metaphorical. INFJs naturally take multiple or creative perspectives on people, situations, and problems. At times there may also be a philosophical, romantic, or even mystical quality to the way their minds work. Introverted intuition gives a certainty to their insights, and with development of extraverted feeling they may work in a determined way to make their visions a reality.

Feeling provides INFJs with a way of giving structure to and critiquing their vision, and thus their visions are often about possibilities for people or for humanity as a whole. Though feeling is important and necessary, intuition is primary for INFJs, and it pulls them to look to patterns and to possibilities. Feeling puts their future-orientation in a people context, and thus issues of self-realization and human development are often of great import to INFJs. They are usually concerned in an ongoing way not only with their own growth but with the growth of others as well.

INFJs are deeply concerned with fellowship and harmony, and with development of feeling, they are caring and compassionate. They are concerned with what is good for people, and they often see people's hidden beauty. INFJs can be exquisitely empathic, and their sensitivity may almost border on the psychic; at times they may even feel a need to shut out their perceptions of what others are experiencing. With developed empathic skills, INFJs can become powerful and dramatically insightful helpers of others, and indeed they are often found in the fields of psychology, spirituality, education, or in the helping professions.

INFJs usually have a love of learning and they are typically academically inclined. No matter what their field, their great powers of concentration can make them excellent researchers. INFJs need to find a place in the world where their unique gifts can be expressed and used, and they may feel like outsiders in a society that does not have a clear place for those with their unique blend of gifts. They need work that provides opportunities to make use of their creativity, insight, and ability to organize. In their work, INFJs are willing to take on responsibility, and they complete tasks through their quiet perseverance. They may be a behind-the-scenes person who drives and gets things done, or with good development of extraverted feeling, they may be found in positions of leadership. INFJs win followers through magnetism and harmony, through quiet firmness and through a deep-felt belief in their insights. Their certainty of the truth of their intuitions also leads to their developing a strong sense of independence.

INFJs are often quiet observers of people and the human condition. They have an ability to capture the essence of an interaction, a people situation, and to be aware of the timeless qualities of the human condition. With artistic or creative interests (which they often have), they may express these insights in art or writing. INFJs often have facility with the written or spoken word, and with foreign languages, and reading is usually a source of great joy for them.

In relationships, INFJs can be quiet and insightful friends. Idealists at heart, they greatly value trust and authenticity in relationships. At times, however, others may experience them as certain of—or even stubborn about—their own correctness. Though they typically are concerned with maintaining harmonious relationships and with pleasing others, INFJs may be surprised to hear that others view them as pushy or controlling. Others may also experience them as hard to know or easily hurt, and confrontations and conflict can indeed be terribly painful for INFJs. They are private individuals who may share only a small portion of their inner world with others, not only because they may have difficulty verbalizing their inner experiences, but because they believe others may not understand their insights.

INFJs need development of extraverted feeling to tell them which of their visions or dreams are the most important to pursue. Without that development, they may have difficulty hearing feedback or alternative views from others, and they may neglect to attend to outside realities that contradict their inner vision. Development of feeling and a willingness to move into action will help INFJs avoid becoming trapped in their inner visions of the possibilities, with no way of bringing them into fruition in the pragmatic

world. In other words, their dreams and plans will stay just those: dreams and plans. With maturity, INFJs are also able to take in new information and change their stance if they see the need for doing so. Development of thinking and sensing will help them take a hard-nosed look at how they can translate their inner images into outer realities.

Under stress, INFJs may compulsively attempt to organize their outer world but achieve no real embodiment of their visions and ideals. They may also be or appear to be surprisingly critical, perfectionistic, or moralistic. Under stress INFJs may also become self-absorbed in their inner world, have difficulty articulating their needs, and become exceptionally self-critical. Under extreme stress they may become overinvolved in physical experiences (too much exercise), or neglect their physical experience (eat too little), or they may possibly drive themselves to exhaustion.

Key words

vision ■ insight ■ creativity ■ harmony
sensitivity ■ growth ■ language ■ metaphor ■ symbols ■ quiet intensity

INTJ
Introverted Intuition with
Extraverted Thinking

For INTJs t

he dominant force in their lives is their attention to the inner world of possibilities, symbols, abstractions, images, and thoughts. Insight in conjunction with logical analysis is the essence of their approach to the world; they think systemically. Ideas are the substance of life for INTJs and they have a driving need to understand, to know, and to demonstrate competence in their areas of interest. INTJs inherently trust their insights, and with their task-orientation will work intensely to make their visions into realities.

Knowing by way of insight is paramount for INTJs. They want to make sense of the world. To learn, to absorb, and to press the limits of their knowledge are the goals of the INTJ. They are not afraid to think any thought, knowing that all ideas need not be applied or acted upon. They naturally find relationships among disparate theories and systems of knowledge. They want, indeed *must*, see the big picture.

INTJs value logic, but are primarily driven by insight/intuition. Ideas, images, thoughts, and insights emerge spontaneously into their awareness, and only then do they try to make some sense of them using thinking. Their bias in problem solving is to allow the mind to roam freely. Their insights can give them a sense of certainty, and they may appear stubborn. With self-awareness, INTJs are open to new information, though the certainty with which they speak may bar others from trying to argue with them or to provide them with new information. INTJs are willing and able to learn from any source, regardless of status; they are also willing to question ideas, regardless of their source.

Thinking provides the logical analysis to give form and order to the substances generated by the INTJ's inner insight. Thinking helps them critique their visions, but thinking is always secondary to the drive to attend to their intuitive perception. Thinking in conjunction with intuition gives their thinking a systemic quality and they enjoy solving complex problems. They naturally see the world in multiple perspectives, all of which may be seen as true. INTJs mentally play out possible scenarios to determine the consequences of various courses of action; they are the ultimate strategists. They love theory, and they also want to get things done. Ideas are to be implemented, and because they believe in the truth of their insights, INTJs will work tirelessly to turn what is possible into what is real.

INTJs want and need challenge, and they often have a high need for achievement. They have a driving need to be competent, and they often set high standards for themselves. They cannot *not* critique their own behavior and performance; they are always analyzing their own actions with an eye to improvement, whether they are at work or at play. With such high expectations of themselves, they can be quite self-critical. They can also be very impatient with error, inefficiency, and lack of competence, in themselves, in systems, and in others. Whether the focus of their attention is an idea, a person, a product, or a system, INTJs are constantly thinking of improvement.

Looking into the future, seeing trends, and engaging in long-range planning are often areas of interest and skill for INTJs. They tend to keep thoughts and insights to themselves, unless sharing is needed to bring a vision to fruition. It is more important to INTJs to understand other people than to direct them, though they can and will direct others if it is needed. Willpower is of great importance to them, and they believe they can achieve their goals through its application.

INTJs often have interests in scientific and theoretical pursuits, but may have interests in any field where wide-ranging thought is required. With academic interests, they may be excellent teachers and researchers. With business interests, and with their eye to systems and improvement, they are often found in management and planning. Intuition often gives their thinking a philosophical or artistic quality, and INTJs may in fact have interests in philosophy or art. They are driven to be creative whatever their field of interest, and once they have developed and implemented a system, the routine becomes boring and they must either change the system or move on to something new.

INTJs have an exceptionally strong need for independence. They want a problem to solve or a project to complete, and they don't want too many instructions. Authority and hierarchy are understood, and seen as necessary at times, but INTJs are skeptical and willing to question the actions of anyone in that hierarchy. Respect is given to others only on the basis of their competence and understanding, not on the basis of their position. When INTJs are certain of their insights, they will ignore the system and rules.

In relationships, INTJs tend to be quiet and reserved, and they often manifest a cool self-confidence. In general their exterior expression is controlled and little leaks through; as a result they may appear interpersonally distant. Because they also tend to be analytical and by nature to question things, INTJs can appear challenging and insensitive. They may indeed neglect to attend to feeling and relationship issues, and forget to express appreciation or empathy when these are needed. However, INTJs are usually much more approachable and open than they appear on the outside.

Development of extraverted thinking will provide INTJs with a tool for critiquing their insights and ideas. Otherwise they may end up trapped in their visions of the possibilities, with no way for determining which are the best options or ideas to pursue. INTJs are in danger of becoming over-involved in reflection and/or hairsplitting, and thus they may fail to move into action. Development of thinking as well as sensing will help them avoid this pitfall and also help them find ways to implement their ideas. They could also benefit from learning to express appreciation to others, and from attending to what they themselves and others feel or care about.

Under stress, INTJs may become over-structured and lose the ability to respond flexibly to the outer world. They may also become paralyzed by their ability to take multiple viewpoints and become bogged down in planning stages, seeking perfection before action is ever taken; as a result, their plans may never materialize. Under extreme stress, INTJs can become obsessed with mundane and irrelevant details; they may also become overinvolved in physical experiences (too much exercise), or neglect their physical experience (eat too little).

Key words

vision ▪ insight ▪ understanding

learning ▪ systemic ▪ global ▪ improvement ▪ achievement ▪ competence

ISTP
Introverted Thinking with
Extraverted Sensing

For ISTPs the driving force in their lives is to understand how things and phenomena in the real world work so they can make the best and most effective use of them. They are logical and realistic people, and they are natural troubleshooters. When not actively solving a problem, ISTPs are quiet and analytical observers of their environment, and they naturally look for the underlying sense to any facts they have gathered. ISTPs often pursue variety and even excitement in their hands-on experiences. Although they do have a spontaneous, even playful side, what people often first encounter with them is their detached pragmatism.

ISTPs are logical and analytical people who believe things in the world should make sense. As quiet and realistic observers of the world, they are intensely curious. ISTPs seek experience in the outer world, and they boil that experience down so they can understand the underlying principles of how things work. ISTPs strive for an objective understanding of things not solely for the sake of understanding, but because they want to use things effectively. They love solving hands-on problems.

ISTPs are naturally critical and come to logical conclusions easily, but since their thinking is brought to bear primarily on their inner world of ideas, others may not see the results of these analyses unless the ISTP chooses to share them. What others typically first encounter with them is their active involvement in the outer world of the senses and their tolerant and easy-going approach to life. Their attitude toward life is playful at times, and when they move into action, ISTPs are spontaneous and flexible, even impulsive. When their principles or independent lifestyle are trod upon, however, they can surprise others by becoming quite firm and possibly stubborn.

Sensing provides ISTPs with a way to stay open to new information, but the gathering of information is always secondary to their need to make sense of things. Their prefer-ence for sensing data means that their analysis is brought to bear on the objects, events, and people of the real world, and their thinking tends to be concrete and pragmatic. Thinking in conjunction with sensing also tends to make ISTPs utilitarian; if something cannot be used, than it tends to be of less interest to them. Too much abstraction or theory can frustrate them. In contrast, they do appreciate and have a good memory for factual information. ISTPs tend also to be task-oriented rather than people-oriented and are usually more interested in organizing data or objects than either people or circumstances.

Stimulation of the senses, and sensual experience in general, is of great importance to ISTPs. They often value their material possessions and may also love the outdoors. Having a low tolerance for boredom, ISTPs will pursue excitement and often create action if none is to be found. They enjoy physical activity just for the sheer joy of living in their bodies in the here-and-now. ISTPs may be highly skilled athletes and it is not unusual for them to like adventurous or risky sports. They enjoy honing their ability to respond to the needs of the moment. They are good in crises, and they may also be excellent troubleshooters. ISTPs can be naturals for work in emergency services.

ISTPs often have not only an acute bodily intelligence but a magnificent ability with physical tools and instruments, whether the tool is a computer, a car, or a football. Precision in action and skilled operation of the environment are things to be admired, particularly technical skill, and ISTPs are often mechanically minded. They use their analysis and natural understanding of the world to achieve maximum effect from their efforts; they seek efficiency. In their work, they like to see some kind of tangible result, and thus they are often found in engineering or construction. Since ISTPs often have a very hands-on learning style, traditional class-rooms may hold little interest for them. If they can see the practical application of an idea and can learn in a more active way, they will continue in school.

ISTPs are quite independent, and do not have a great deal of appreciation for rules and regulations. What they do respect are skill, logic, and the ability to respond effectively to problems. Competition is certainly not foreign to ISTPs, and they enjoy responding in more "effective" ways than their competitors. They are commonly found in police work, business, and other areas where this need can be met. They are also found in law, computer programming, and accounting, or any career where they can bring logical order to a mass of facts. Whatever their career, ISTPs need variety and opportunities to learn and to apply their skills. Since they often enjoy solitary activities and hobbies, they also need a career where some in-depth interest can be used.

In relating to others, ISTPs often have a reserved and detached style. ISTPs can be tough-minded and a bit cool; they tend to control their emotions, and little leaks out. They may even be shy, but once they know you, they can be quite playful. Much of their expression is nonverbal, because to ISTPs, actions speak louder than words, and when they do express themselves verbally, they tend to be matter-of-fact. They prefer relationships that are collegial, and since they respect skill in others, they often build relationships around shared activities (e.g., scuba diving). ISTPs may frustrate others with their strong needs for independence and freedom. They resist feeling controlled, which may at times manifest as a lack of commitment, or lack of follow-through.

Development of extraverted sensing will help ISTPs stay open to new information that can be processed using their logical thinking. Without that development, they may get tangled in the world of logic, become certain of the truth of their conclusions, and be unwilling to check out whether or not their "truths" apply to what is really happening in the world outside of their own minds. ISTPs can benefit from learning to establish long-term goals and from adhering to the commitments they make. With maturity, they will also be less inclined to put off decisions. Since ISTPs may sometimes be insensitive to others' needs for feedback and appreciation, they can be seen as unapproachable. Development of feeling will help them attend more to personal and interpersonal issues, including their impact on others, as well as to what others and they themselves care about.

Under stress, ISTPs can feel suddenly trapped or bound by rules or expectations, at which point they may impulsively move out of the constricting situation. In addition, they may become cynical and see only negative possibilities for the future, and as a result put off decisions. Under stress, ISTPs can feel cut off from others, and misinterpret comments made by others as intentionally hurtful. In surprising contrast to their reserved and cool style, under great stress they may even have out-of-proportion explosions of emotion.

Key words

logical ■ analytical ■ adaptable ■ pragmatic
problem-solver ■ troubleshooter ■ adventurous ■ cool ■ independent

ISFP
Introverted Feeling with Extraverted Sensing

For ISFPs the dominant quality in their lives is a deep-felt caring for living things, combined with a quietly playful and sometimes adventurous approach to life and all its experiences. ISFPs typically show their caring in very practical ways, since they often prefer action to words. Their warmth and concern are generally not expressed openly, and what people often first encounter with ISFPs is their quiet adaptability, realism, and "free spirit" spontaneity.

ISFPs deeply value people, relationships, and all of life. Given the ISFP's reflective nature, other people may not see this intense caring until they know the ISFP well. They are compassionate people who are typically sensitive to the emotional states and suffering of others. ISFPs are perhaps the gentlest and kindest of the types; they tend to be acutely aware of nonverbal messages, and their kindness is often expressed in nonverbal ways. Thus they often have a strong affinity with children and animals. They may also have a love of natural things: plants and bodies of water.

ISFPs are idealistic and would like their work to contribute to people in some way: to their comfort, their freedom, their safety. ISFPs also take a very personal approach to life, and it is important for them to find work about which they can care deeply. When they find people about whom they care, they are intensely and fiercely loyal.

ISFPs are deeply concerned with harmony; they like for their relationships and environment to feel comfortable and free from strife. Since disharmony can be very painful to them, they may act as peacemakers in relationships or groups. If disharmony cannot be resolved, they may choose to go their own way. ISFPs are cooperative by nature because they deeply understand that connection and caring are essential to the natural order of the world.

Sensing provides ISFPs with a good grasp of realities and provides them with a way to stay open to new information, though their dominant drive is still a deep process of valuing. ISFPs are usually down-to-earth people who enjoy living in the here and now. They are immersed in the ongoing richness of sensory and sensual experience, and they tend to have a playfully optimistic approach to everyday life. As pragmatists, ISFPs prefer the concrete over the abstract, and they often have a good memory for factual detail. Theory tends to hold little interest for them, and they are more interested in how to make something work than in why it works. Sensing also ensures that their caring is practical; they want to help people in hands-on ways.

ISFPs need freedom and variety in their lives, and they may have a low tolerance for boredom or constrictions. Excitement and adventure often call them, and they want to pursue things at their own pace, and in their own way. They *will* fulfill their commitments to people and institutions, but they do not have a great appreciation for organizational structures in and of themselves. In their spontaneity, ISFPs are often good at responding to the needs of the moment. This is particularly true where a pragmatic response is required: helping a person by making them comfortable, by negotiating a dispute, or by keeping their own head in an emergency. In general, ISFPs are flexible and tolerant; however, when a deep value is violated, they can become quite stubborn, much to the surprise of others.

ISFPs are often excited by action for the sake of action. This often shows as a love of sports, crafts, or other hands-on activities. In fact, ISFPs often have athletic interests, and surprisingly, can be quite competitive in this arena, though it may not be obvious. With their immersion in hands-on activity, they may also develop craftsmanlike skill in their manipulation of athletic equipment, tools, or other instruments.

The ISFP's acute sensitivity to color, sound, and atmosphere may manifest itself as a sense of style and aesthetics. These qualities in conjunction with their discerning attention to sensory data can result in ISFPs being excellent craftworkers, artists, or designers; it is not unusual for ISFPs to have interests in art, music, or dance.

The traditional classroom may have little of interest to ISFPs, particularly as the emphasis on theory increases and opportunities for applications or hands-on learning decrease. When they do enjoy school, it is often because they have found teachers with whom they feel a connection. ISFPs often like to work alone and may despair of finding their place in the world. Without planning, they may indeed drift from one career to another. They *can* find a place, however, and are commonly found in hands-on caring and helping careers, such as health care. ISFPs are also found in business and in technical, trade, or crafts careers, where their pragmatic adaptability can be readily applied.

ISFPs are caring and trusting people, if somewhat reserved. Their warmth becomes apparent once a relationship is established, and they deeply value their friendships. They prefer expression through action and artistry rather than through words, and thus their speech may be short and terse. Since they tend not to blow their own horns, ISFPs can also appear modest. In the extreme, this may become shyness or nonassertiveness, and ISFPs can be in danger of underselling themselves, even though they have so much to offer. They do want to be appreciated for their contributions, as they appreciate others for theirs. If they do not get that acknowledgment, they are in danger of withdrawing.

ISFPs need development of extraverted sensing to ensure that they move into action on their ideals, otherwise they may end up feeling trapped in painful disillusionment. This situation worsens if their idealism becomes extreme perfectionism; nothing meets the ideal. Feeling can give ISFPs a sense of certainty about their evaluation of a situation, and development of sensing will help them stay open to facts from the outer world. Development of sensing will also provide them with information on how to move into action on their ideals. At times, ISFPs may also have difficulty in making decisions, meeting deadlines, or following through. As they learn to use thinking and intuition to look to the future, they will see the long-term consequences of some of these actions. They will also increasingly find their place in the world and find work that contributes in the way they would like.

Under stress ISFPs may lose their self-confidence, become passive, and withdraw. They may also take their resistance to rules and regulations to the extreme and neglect their responsibilities, even ones they care about. Under stress, ISFPs can also and become overly sensitive to the remarks of others and become very self-critical; under extreme stress they may even become surprisingly and outwardly critical of others.

Key words

gentle ■ caring ■ compassionate
modest ■ aesthetic ■ artistic ■ idealistic ■ joyful action

INFP
Introverted Feeling with
Extraverted Intuition

For INFPs the dominant quality in their lives is a deep-felt caring and idealism about people. They experience this intense caring most often in their relationships with others, but they may also experience it around ideas, projects, or any involvement they see as important. INFPs are often skilled communicators, and they are naturally drawn to ideas that embody a concern for human potential. INFPs live in the inner world of values and ideals, but what people often first encounter with them in the outer world is their adaptability and concern for possibilities.

For INFPs, the world and events are viewed from a very personal and often idealistic perspective. INFPs pursue their ideals, and their desire to find their place in the world and express who they are can take on an almost quest-like quality. INFPs look for meaning; they look for it in their lives, in their work, and in their relationships with others. They may feel a strong need to contribute something of importance to the world or to have an impact on the lives of those about whom they care, though they can also be quiet observers of people and humanity at large.

People and relationships are what the world is about, and harmony in relationships is of great importance to the INFP. They are very concerned with the impact of their decisions on individuals, not only on those about whom they care but on themselves and on their own values as well. Their deep need and desire for harmony can sometimes show as a concern with keeping peace, and with maturity, they are open-minded and egalitarian. INFPs have a desire for harmony which may at times get in the way of their getting their own needs met. Their caring, warmth, and deep valuing of relationships are also difficult to communicate to others and may not be immediately apparent to people in their lives. INFPs may even appear a bit cool or aloof from the outside, though they would be surprised that others experience them in this way, given the warmth and loyalty they feel inside.

Intuition gives their feeling a future focus and orients INFPs to the abstract and symbolic. Intuition, however, is always secondary to the deep-felt valuing and caring that characterizes their feeling. Their orientation to the future sometimes finds expression in their desire to help others manifest their potential. Their intuition may also find embodiment in creative activity or show itself as an interest in communication. INFPs often have a gift for the written or spoken word, and they typically have a sense of nuance of meaning. INFPs want the freedom to live their ideals, and they do like variety in their lives.

If interested, INFPs may find an outlet for their gifts in the fields of writing, journalism, or foreign languages. Their ideas and their writing are conceptual and metaphorical, with a concern for universals and values, but their writing also tends to have a warm personal tone. Many INFPs also have a deep love and enjoyment of reading. On a subject about which they care, and on which they have had time to reflect, they can be exceptionally verbal and persuasive.

Since creativity is often of importance to INFPs, they may have artistic interests or a concern for aesthetics. They attend to style as well as content in their creative expression, and their creativity is often a vehicle for communicating their values and ideals. INFPs may be strongly attracted to, and enjoy experiencing, the human condition in all its joys and sadnesses, as represented in the works of artists, musicians, writers, and film-makers through history.

INFPs are excited by new ideas and new possibilities, particularly as they may find expression in people's lives. As a result INFPs are often drawn to areas like counseling, where they can use their caring and grasp of the possible. With interests in academics they may be found in the fields of literature, psychology, and the arts and sciences. Spirituality can also play a large role in their lives, as they look for a personal connection to something larger than themselves. Though INFPs care about people, they are often drawn to fields where they can work independently. Their behavior in the outer world is usually characterized by flexibility and they may be frustrated by routine, structure, and rules.

In their relationships, INFPs are often adaptable people who quietly manifest compassion and sensitivity. Their sensitivity may be seen in their intense empathic responses to the joys and suffering of others, and to those in need. Commitment, loyalty, and love are often of great importance to them, as are family and children. Interestingly, they may be in love with the idea of love, and without maturity, they may become passive and fail to move into compassionate and caring action. Though INFPs often have a strong sense of what is right and wrong, outwardly they are very tolerant; they will, however, let you know if you have trod on their values. Without development, an INFP may fail to express his or her needs clearly, and thus others may be confused or frustrated by not knowing they have violated something of importance to the INFP.

Development of extraverted intuition is necessary for INFPs to help them stay open to new ideas, new information, and new experiences. Otherwise they may feel deeply, but never move into action, or they may fail to check whether their beliefs about people are

true. As a result, their strong sense of right and wrong can lead to their being perceived as moralistic by others. Development of intuition will also give INFPs possible ways to pursue their ideals. Without this development, INFPs' energies may become trapped inside, squandered on worrying about meaningless issues, or brought to bear on issues that are so big that they do not know where to start or how to have an impact. Development of sensing and thinking will also help them take a hard real-world look at their plans, and give them the firmness needed to manifest their ideals.

Because INFPs are often attracted to new possibilities, and because they may have difficulty saying no, they may bite off more than they can chew. They can have too many projects going to successfully complete any of them. Under stress, they may also become rigid and perfectionistic, feel inadequate, and become critical of themselves. Under extreme stress, and in surprising contrast to their tolerant and caring style, they may even become outwardly critical of others, feeling that others are failing to meet the ideals the INFP has set for them.

Key words

deep-felt valuing ■ quiet caring ■ relationships
harmony ■ meaning ■ ideals ■ artistic ■ symbols ■ metaphors ■ writing

INTP
Introverted Thinking with
Extraverted Intuition

For INTPs the driving force in their lives is to understand whatever phenomenon is the focus of their attention. They want to make sense of the world—as a concept—and they often enjoy opportunities to be creative. INTPs are logical, analytical, and detached in their approach to the world; they naturally question and critique ideas and events as they strive for understanding. INTPs usually have little need to control the outer world, or to bring order to it, and they often appear very flexible and adaptable in their lifestyle.

Logic and analysis are paramount for INTPs. They have a drive to analyze, to understand, and to make sense of ideas and events; things simply must make sense, and they *should*. In fact, their internal juggling of ideas almost has a life of its own. INTPs think naturally in terms of cause and effect and logical consequences. They look for the underlying principles that explain the nature of the world or for the principles that capture the essence of their area of interest; INTPs enjoy solving complex problems.

INTPs are naturally skeptical and critical. They question, question, and question some more. As a result, they may appear to others to be challenging, though they do not intend to criticize others. Because they value precision, INTPs are simply looking for logical inconsistencies in writing, speech, thought, and ideas. Exactness in definitions is of great importance to them, and without restraint they may engage in unnecessary hairsplitting. INTPs may also have dramatic powers of concentration, and in using these they may develop an amazingly deep and complex understanding of some area(s) of interest. In fact, they may become so involved in the inner world and in their subject of interest that they may forget about the passage of time.

Intuition orients the INTP's thinking to the future, and to the abstract and symbolic, but intuition is always subordinate to the need to analyze and understand ideas and events. New ideas and new ways of doing things fascinate INTPs. In fact, they are infinitely curious: about ideas, books, systems of thought, computers, or any other current area of interest. They may use their logic and intuition to develop new and highly intricate systems of thought, and thus they can be brilliant and innovative thinkers. INTPs are organizers in the world of abstract ideas; they view things systemically and creatively. They want the freedom to pursue their ideas in their own way, and thus they seek variety and independence in their lives.

INTPs may have scientific, theoretical, or artistic interests, and can be found in computer, physical, or social sciences. They may be teachers, researchers, or thinkers in any field in which abstract and complex thought is required, as in philosophy. For INTPs, experience provides data, and the data is then analyzed for its fit into the complex mental models that they have been developing, possibly over a lifetime. The model is often more important than the experience itself, and INTPs are usually more interested in understanding and solving abstract problems than in the actual application of their ideas. They need to find a career where a deep and intensive understanding of some subject is important.

INTPs are often nontraditional. Their questioning attitude and need for autonomy may even lead to their being or appearing iconoclastic. They do, however, value intelligence and prize competence. INTPs give respect to others based on others' perceived competence and depth of understanding rather than on the basis of position or external trappings of power. This is a natural extension of their strong valuing of autonomy. They are usually tolerant and adaptable and give other people wide leeway of behavior, feeling little need to control others. However, when the INTP's principles (which may not be immediately apparent) are violated, he or she can be seen as very firm, even stubborn.

INTPs are usually more interested in ideas and concepts than in people, though people may certainly be the subject of their acute thinking and analysis. A consequence of this detached and analytical orientation is that INTPs may miss interpersonal nuances, not appreciate the need for social niceties, and end up in hot water as a result. They can appear reserved and impersonal, though they do usually enjoy discussions with other people who share their own keen interest in ideas. Additionally, INTPs may be insensitive to the emotional needs of others and others may see them as aloof or unapproachable. At worst they may be or appear to be arrogant and critical.

Without development of their extraverted intuition, INTPs may remain aloof and incomprehensible, unable to work out or apply their ideas in the outside world. Development of their intuition will also help them take in information that can be processed using their logical thinking. Without that development, INTPs may become entangled in the inner world of logical thoughts and systems, and become too distant from the outer world of people and action. As a result, they may become certain of the truth of their logic, but be unwilling to check whether their "truths" apply to what is really happening in the world outside of their own minds. By attending only to what is logical, INTPs may also forget to attend to what is important to *them* as people. They may at times be weak on follow-through and self-direction, and they may even forget to attend to the details of everyday life. Appropriate development of sensing and feeling will help them avoid these traps as well as help them give greater attention to interpersonal issues.

Under stress, INTPs may feel overwhelmed and misunderstood. However, because they are so adaptable they may remain in a situation rather than leave it or negotiate a change. They may also feel confused when people in general or significant others don't behave "logically." INTPs need to understand that relationships have a logic of their own that the INTP may neglect to register as valid or important. Under great stress, and in contrast to their usual calm cool style, they may erupt with out-of-proportion expressions of emotion, particularly in response to relationship stresses.

Key words

logical ■ conceptual ■ analytical

objective ■ critical ■ ingenious ■ complex ■ creative ■ curious ■ ideas

ESTP
Extraverted Sensing with
Introverted Thinking

For ESTPs the dominant quality in their lives is their enthusiastic attention to the outer world of hands-on and real-life experiences. ESTPs are excited by continuous involvement in new activities and in the pursuit of new challenges. They tend to be logical and analytical in their approach to life, and they have an acute sense of how objects, events, and people in the world work. ESTPs are typically energetic and adaptable realists, who prefer to experience and accept life rather than to judge or organize it.

ESTPs are spontaneous and fun-loving realists. They move into action easily, even impulsively. ESTPs live for excitement, pursuing new involvements, new relationships, and new locales. They live in the here and now and are most effective and happy when they can act on the needs of the moment. Flexibility is their hallmark. ESTPs do not have a lot of "shoulds" in their lives. As a result they tend to be tolerant and open to a variety of experiences and people.

ESTPs playfully seek out physical experience in all of its forms, in new food or travel, for example. In fact, things physical are usually of great interest to ESTPs, and they often have the latest electronics, vehicles, tools, and clothes. They may also have a taste for aesthetics. As keen observers of the outer world, ESTPs may have an excellent memory for facts, details, and what is literally happening in their environment. Conversely, abstractions tend to be of little interest to them, and they may not entirely trust theory. In fact, they often learn best by optimistically diving into the middle of things and getting their hands on whatever it is that needs to be learned.

ESTPs are often excited by the sheer joy of activity. For example, they may enjoy participating in a sport for its own sake, their expertise arising from immersion in the action rather than from a focus on achievement. Incidentally, participation in sports or other forms of exercise often provides them with great pleasure and they may be gifted athletes. With their needs for variety and freedom, ESTPs can become frustrated by too much structure and may at times go around regulations they find too constricting.

Thinking gives ESTPs a way to critique and give meaning to their experiences, and to order their perceptions of reality, but thinking is always secondary to the drive to gain new experiences. Thinking puts their pragmatism in a logical context; they look for the principles that underlie the working of things in the real world. As realists, ESTPs accept facts as they are, but because they are adaptable, they also know that there are many ways to solve a problem. With their unbending faith in their ability to respond to the needs of the moment, ESTPs are often skilled at managing crises or at solving real-life problems; they can make excellent negotiators and troubleshooters. They can also be tough-minded and a bit cool by nature, in spite of their outgoing personality.

ESTPs are pragmatists at heart. They want to concretely address the *actual* issue or problem at hand. As a result, the traditional classroom tends to hold little of interest to ESTPs, and the more the focus is on theory, the more quickly will their interest be lost. They may literally have trouble sitting still in class. They want to learn how to do something, and they want to learn by doing it, rather than by reading or talking about it; actions speak louder than words. For ESTPs to maintain their interest in school, they need to find active ways to learn and applications for the ideas they are studying.

ESTPs can have magnificent hands-on skills in using the tool of their choice, whether it be a computer, a golf club, a motorcycle, or anything else. As skilled operators of their environment, ESTPs know what resources are available and how to make the best use of them to achieve an end. This skillful operation may also show as an orientation to the arts or crafts, and they can be quite mechanically minded. Whatever the domain, ESTPs prefer working with things that can be seen, and thus are often found in the engineering, construction, technical, and health care or fitness professions.

Adventure, risk, and competition are not

foreign to ESTPs, and they enjoy the thrill of responding in more "effective" ways than an opponent. As a result, ESTPs are commonly found in police work, business, and other areas where this need can be met, and where they can demonstrate the skillfulness and even-headedness they so value. They also like to have an impact on others, and since they may also enjoy being "on stage," they can be found working as entertainers, promoters, marketers, and salespeople.

ESTPs are usually seen as friendly, casual, and experienced in life. When they choose to be, they *can* be very perceptive of other people's attitudes and beliefs. However, their preference for matter-of-factness in communications may at times be experienced as tactlessness. Whatever their area of interest, they usually have an enthusiasm that can energize those around them. They are naturals at parties, and can be excellent at group work. Though typically good-natured, ESTPs can engage in one-upmanship. In the extreme, this playful quality can wear on acquaintances, and at worst they may be perceived as manipulative. Since ESTPs also value their sense of freedom, others may at times experience them as lacking commitment in relationships.

Development of introverted thinking will help ESTPs focus, define, and adhere to goals, and help them determine which of their interests are the most important to pursue. In general, ESTPs can benefit from a greater appreciation of the need for structure and follow-through. Setting standards for themselves will also help them avoid the trap of indiscriminately pursuing experiences simply for the sake of excitement. If they find that too many of their decisions are based on the needs of the moment, they may benefit from making longer range plans. They may also benefit from attending to the impact of their behavior on others and remembering that there is more to relationships than people's ability to have a good time together.

Under stress ESTPs may become excessively impulsive, stubbornly ignoring structures, commitments, and deadlines. They may also pursue exciting new experiences at the cost of career and relationships. Under great stress, ESTPs may blow details out of proportion, imagining that they have the worst possible meaning, and see only the negatives in the future. In contrast to their usually confident and adaptable style, they may feel confused, latch onto one *possible* interpretation of their problems and be *certain* it is correct, and ignore all data to the contrary.

Key words

excitement ■ risk ■ pragmatic ■ realistic ■ adaptable
troubleshooter ■ spontaneous ■ active ■ impulsive ■ enthusiastic

ESFP
Extraverted Sensing with
Introverted Feeling

For ESFPs the dominant quality in their lives is their enthusiastic attention to the outer world of hands-on and real-life experiences. ESFPs are excited by continuous involvement in new activities and new relationships. They also have a deep concern for people, and they show their caring in warm and pragmatic gestures of helping. ESFPs are typically energetic and adaptable realists, who prefer to experience and accept life rather than to judge or organize it.

ESFPs are energetic, fun-loving realists. They seek fun and excitement and will create them if they are nowhere to be found. ESFPs love life and take obvious joy in drinking it to the full; they continually seek new experiences, new involvements, new friends. Since ESFPs rely heavily on their experience in their understanding and decision making, the more experiences they have, the better! They are more interested in gathering new experiences than in critiquing or evaluating them. Since they seek to know rather than to judge, they tend also to be open to and tolerant of a wide variety of people and activities.

ESFPs are spontaneous, flexible, and playful, and they love activity in and of itself. For example, they can enjoy participating in a sport for its own sake. It is the action itself that is fun, rather than any drive to improve their performance. Incidentally, participation in sports or other forms of exercise often provides ESFPs with great pleasure and they may be gifted athletes.

ESFPs move into action because that is what life is all about, and they easily respond to the needs of the here and now. Above all else, they are adaptable. In fact, they like a bit of adventure in their lives, and in their work too if possible. ESFPs are often good at handling crises, and thus they can make very effective troubleshooters. They tend to be casual, and may be frustrated by too many rules and regulations. If rules disturb them too much, they will often find ways around them.

ESFPs swim in a sea of sensory experience and thus they often are masters of factual data, noticing and remembering details and specifics. With their immersion in what is real, and in their pursuit of new experience, ESFPs often want to try out the newest fashions, the newest electronics, the newest anything. They appreciate and enjoy their material possessions.

They are also pragmatists at heart. ESFPs are more interested in if and how something can be used, rather than in "why" it works. They are more interested in application than in theory, and in facts than in abstractions. ESFPs tend to have less interest in book learning just for the sake of gathering knowledge, and they usually have a keen common sense.

Feeling provides ESFPs with a way of bringing order to their lives and experiences, but feeling is always secondary to the drive to have new experiences and the rush to be involved in new hands-on activities. Feeling places their pragmatism in a people context; ESFPs like to help and support others in very practical ways. They care about people, and relationships mean much to them. There is a very warm and personal touch in all that they do. When ESFPs make decisions, they are concerned with the impact of those decisions on people, as well as on their own sense of self. They want harmony and tend to be non-competitive people. They may even be skilled at negotiating a common ground between those in conflict.

Since the traditional classroom does not provide as many opportunities as ESFPs would prefer for hands-on learning, they may not enjoy it very much. As they move to higher and higher levels of education, they tend to lose interest with the increasing focus on theory and abstractions. Thus they must find a practical reason and application for what they are learning to get them to continue. ESFPs want to learn by doing, and by being with others who are doing what the ESFP wants to learn.

In general, ESFPs demonstrate their caring for others in very practical ways; they *show* their concern and help others out in direct fashion. For example, they are more likely to give a cold person a blanket than to give them directions to a warmer state.

ESFPs can also be quite empathic, and they often have a special concern for children, animals, and all things natural. As a result, they are often found in helping, teaching, and service careers, and within these careers they tend to work in the hands-on areas. For example, in the helping careers ESFPs are often found in nursing or family medicine, and in the teaching careers they are often found teaching K-12.

With their outgoing nature, ESFPs are also found in business, sales, and entertainment. Whatever their interests, they want and need careers where they have a lot of opportunities to meet and be with others. They are naturals for working in groups, and are usually skilled and comfortable communicators who may be quite persuasive.

ESFPs are people people. They seek company and others seek them out. ESFPs are friendly and enthusiastic, even sparkling. They are often the life of the party, and others can get caught up in their excitement and optimism. Their spontaneity can sometimes manifest as impulsiveness, and though they are caring and generous, ESFPs may frustrate others by what appears to be a lack of interest in adhering to commitments. As social beings, they want and need feedback and appreciation, and they like to give the same to others.

They may be hurt by a lack of positive strokes.

Development of introverted feeling will help ESFPs develop consistency and direction in their lives, and help them determine which of their interests are the most important to pursue. Development of feeling will also help them work on planning and follow-through and in bringing things in their lives to closure. In general ESFPs can benefit from developing a greater appreciation of the need for structures and adherence to obligations. They may also have too much of a concern for here-and-now experience at times. Development of thinking and intuition will help them to look at the longer term consequences of some of their quick actions and to see the need for planning.

Under stress, ESFPs may become excessively impulsive and overcommit without following through. They may also interpret actions and statements made by others too personally and read negative intent between the lines. In contrast to their usual style of pragmatically jumping into action, they may feel trapped in confusion. Under great stress, ESFPs may look to the future with pessimism, and see only negative possibilities, or latch on to one possible negative interpretation of events in their lives.

Key words

hands-on ■ realistic ■ excitement ■ people
social ■ expressive ■ enthusiasm ■ spontaneous ■ impulsive ■ new ■ adaptable

ENFP
Extraverted Intuition with
Introverted Feeling

For ENFPs the dominant quality in their lives is their attention to the outer world of possibilities; they are excited by continuous involvement in anything new, whether it be new ideas, new people, or new activities. Though ENFPs thrive on what is possible and what is new, they also experience a deep concern for people as well. Thus, they are especially interested in possibilities for people. ENFPs are typically energetic, enthusiastic people who lead spontaneous and adaptable lives.

Intuition constantly draws ENFPs to the new. They like, want, even *must* do new things or at least do old things in new ways. This drive arises out of their experience that whatever is over the horizon is always more interesting than what is here and present. ENFPs trust the truth of their intuition and they charge off with excitement and inspiration in whatever direction it points them. With their orientation to the new, they are natural brainstormers, and look to the future with optimism. They are creative, active, and imaginative. ENFPs enjoy starting and becoming involved in the initial stages of a project but usually have less interest in follow-through. They tend to be very spontaneous, flexible, and adaptable people. What may look like difficulty in committing is a manifestation of their desire to miss nothing. After all, deciding prematurely means they might close off many interesting options down the road.

Feeling provides ENFPs with a way to focus and critique their vision, but feeling is always secondary to the driving energy of their intuition. Feeling does often mold their visions into possibilities for people. They are concerned with personal growth, identity, and authenticity, both for themselves and for others. ENFPs want to be free to be themselves, to express themselves, and they want others to feel free to do the same. ENFPs may also be skilled in perceiving what is important to others, and what others are thinking: a valuable skill in any people-oriented profession. They are idealists, believing their vision of the higher possibilities for people are true now or can be made true in short order.

ENFPs want and need involvement with people, and they value harmony in those relationships. They derive great pleasure from meeting and talking with others, and they enjoy opportunities to think out loud. ENFPs are expressive and often have intense emotional responses to happenings and to people in their lives; vital emotional experience is of great importance to them. They like others to be as excited as they are by new ideas and new involvements, and they naturally focus on commonalities in relationships. This focus, in conjunction with their concern for others and their ability to take a global perspective, often leads to skills in negotiation or mediation.

With their combination of intuition and feeling, ENFPs tend to think globally and metaphorically. They are often verbally gifted, particularly in conversation. ENFPs look for the meaning behind statements and events. As a result, they can be skilled integrators of information and ideas, and they are often good at reading between the lines in conversations. They love learning new things, and love looking for new perspectives on facts, events, and people. ENFPs typically learn more by focusing on broad issues and are less concerned with the working out of their ideas.

ENFPs are people people; they are usually gregarious by nature, and they are often performers. They usually have a wide network of friends, acquaintances, and business contacts, and they are naturals for work that requires meeting, persuading, or motivating others. ENFPs are catalysts for change and generators of enthusiasm, and they are often found in counseling, psychology, teaching, the helping professions, or personnel work. ENFPs may also have interests in the humanities and the arts, particularly the dramatic arts. Their adaptability and imagination help them to develop skills in almost any area of interest.

ENFPs are typically intolerant of routine, and they need variety in their work. Their perception of time is open-ended, and they like work that allows them to have a variety of projects going on at once. They need to find a place where they can use their abilities to generate new ideas and to look at things in creative ways. Though they are concerned with people, ENFPs are typically quite independent and tend not to be great upholders of tradition. In fact, it is natural for them to push boundaries and to redefine rules.

ENFPs are usually seen as warm, charming, and friendly. At times, however, others may feel overwhelmed by their energy and excitement. In relationships, they are typically supportive, express appreciation freely, and they like to receive feedback as well. They may, however, be overconcerned with harmony at times. As a result, they may be seen as having difficulty standing their ground or confronting others.

ENFPs need development of introverted feeling to help them choose which exciting possibilities they will focus upon and to help them follow through on their visions. Developing a hierarchy of values will help them clarify a direction in life and help them develop self-discipline. Once a project has started, ENFPs may have difficulty attending to the details: for development they need to realize that implementing an idea is not always as easy as imagining it. ENFPs can also become so excited by a new idea that they may miss cues that others are not as excited by their new interest as they are. Development of feeling will help them avoid this situation. Development of thinking will help them avoid any overconcern with harmony. Development of thinking and sensing will help them attend to the pragmatics of making their visions become realities.

Under stress, ENFPs may have difficulty saying no. Consequently, they may take on too many projects without any practical way of completing them. They can also become rigidly nonconforming if they feel too much structure is being imposed on them. Under extreme stress, ENFPs may also find it difficult to pull themselves away from a project to attend to practical or physical needs. For example, they may forget to eat or sleep, may drive themselves to exhaustion, or may even have inexplicable accidents. In surprising contrast to their usual global style, they can even become compulsively attentive to irrelevant details.

Key words

enthusiastic ■ visionary ■ energetic ■ possibilities ■ new
many ■ people ■ action ■ excitement ■ creative ■ caring ■ warmth

---

ENTP
Extraverted Intuition with
Introverted Thinking

For ENTPs the dominant quality in their lives is their attention to the outer world of possibilities; they are excited by continuous involvement in anything new, whether it be new ideas, new people, or new activities. They look for patterns and meaning in the world, and they often have a deep need to analyze, to understand, and to know the nature of things. ENTPs are typically energetic, enthusiastic people who lead spontaneous and adaptable lives.

ENTPs are continually pulled to new activities, new ways of doing things, and new ways of thinking about things. What is over the horizon is almost always more interesting than what is going on in the here and now. ENTPs can be dynamic visionaries, and they trust the truth of their insights. They believe that if they can imagine something, then materializing it is just one step away. ENTPs work toward their vision or toward solutions in bursts of energy and enthusiasm. They are eternal optimists.

ENTPs are pursuers of change. They are innovators, inventors, planners, and designers. Driven by inspiration, they tend to have a low tolerance for boredom and to become frustrated when things appear to be moving too slowly. They want action and variety in their lives and they typically have many irons in the fire. With their bias toward active learning, ENTPs want to see their visions materialized in the world, though not following through on their visions may at times be their downfall.

Thinking provides ENTPs with a way to focus and critique their visions, but thinking is always secondary to the driving energy of their intuition. Thinking does make them logical and analytical, and thus they value rationality as well as inspiration. Things *should* make sense, and if they don't now, the ENTP believes they *will* eventually after further analytical probing. ENTPs love to solve complex problems and approach them as challenges.

ENTPs continually look for the meaning behind statements, in events, in data, and in actions. They are often skilled at noticing trends and forecasting the future. Natural conceptualizers, they continually build and rebuild mental models to explain the world, and their thinking tends to be complex, abstract, and original. Because ENTPs are also critical in their thinking, they may be skilled in being able to see several different points of view. They imagine the possibilities of a situation and then strategically analyze those different possibilities to determine which course of action would be the most effective to pursue. ENTPs can be ingenious, and they also trust their abilities to improvise and respond to the needs of the moment.

ENTPs tend to value knowledge and competence, and they are often achievement-oriented. As a result, they tend to value others on the basis of perceived intelligence and ability, rather than on the basis of status. ENTPs, however, are often aware of power and status issues. They can play the game if need be to achieve the realization of their visions.

ENTPs enjoy careers that call upon their ability to look at things creatively and analytically. They may also become bored if they do not feel challenged with a continuous stream of new projects. ENTPs are often drawn to the sciences and technology. They may also be entrepreneurs, marketers, or professors, or anything else that engages their interests.

ENTPs tend to be gregarious, sociable people, and they can be quite exciting company. They enjoy being involved with others, and their enthusiasm is contagious. It may also be overwhelming to others at times. Typically easy-going and casual, they usually look self-confident in their interactions with others. ENTPs do tend to view their lives and people in an objective and analytical manner, and as a result they can be or appear to be insensitive to emotional issues or relationship concerns. Paradoxically, they can be skilled at discerning what others think or believe, when they choose to attend to others in that way.

ENTPs are often verbally skilled and can be energetic conversationalists. They may at times argue for the sake of argument, simply because they enjoy the interplay of ideas with another person. Others, however, may be turned off by their penchant for debate and intellectual sparring. ENTPs also tend to have a high need for autonomy. This need, in conjunction with their belief in their own insights, often leads to their being dyed-in-the-wool individualists. They are not strong believers in rules, and they will often ignore or go around structures that make no sense to them.

ENTPs need development of introverted thinking to help them critique their many ideas and inspirations, otherwise they may waste their energy by being involved in too many projects or in an endless succession of new interests. ENTPs need to make use of their ability to analyze to help them clarify a direction in life and to help them develop self-discipline. They need to realize that implementing an idea is not always as easy as imagining it. Often once a project is begun, ENTPs can have difficulty attending to or following through on details. Development of thinking will help them see the consequences of continual pursuit of the new with no follow-through. Through development of feeling, they can become more aware of their impact on others and of the sometimes negative consequences of continual intellectual challenge and debate. Development of sensing will help them attend to the pragmatics of making their visions a reality.

Under stress, ENTPs may take on too many projects without any practical way of completing them. They may even become rigidly nonconforming if they feel too much structure is being imposed on them. Under great stress, ENTPs may find it difficult to pull themselves away from a project to attend to practical or physical needs. For example, they may forget to eat or sleep, may drive themselves to exhaustion, or may even have inexplicable accidents. In surprising contrast to their usual abstract and global style, under stress they can even become compulsively focused on irrelevant details.

Key words

energy ■ enthusiasm ■ new ■ many
abstract ■ theoretical ■ logical ■ complex ■ global ■ entrepreneur

ESTJ
Extraverted Thinking with Introverted Sensing

For ESTJs the driving force in their lives is their need to analyze and bring into logical order the outer world of events, people, and things. ESTJs like to organize anything that comes into their domain, and they will work energetically to complete tasks so they can quickly move from one to the next. Sensing orients their thinking to current facts and realities, and thus gives their thinking a pragmatic quality. ESTJs take their responsibilities seriously and believe others should do so as well.

For the ESTJ, logic and analysis are paramount. They believe the outer world should and will make sense, and they strive to bring that world into logical order. ESTJs believe behavior should be logical, and they work to govern their own behavior by strict principles. They have a strong need to organize the facts, projects, events, or people in their area of influence. Since they love *action*, their organizing has a dynamic quality. ESTJs live for decisions; it feels good to settle things. They would rather be certain and be wrong than be uncertain.

ESTJs readily apply their clear standards of what is correct and right to what goes on around them. With their extraverted thinking, they will openly critique anyone or anything that does not meet the standard, but they do so only with the purpose of bringing people and procedures back into a rational and natural order. ESTJs apply standards and measures to themselves and to others only to increase the efficiency and effectiveness they so deeply value. They willingly supervise others to ensure goals are met, whether the goals are those of the community, organization, business, family, or group.

ESTJs naturally gravitate toward management and other administrative or leadership positions. With the sense of certainty their extraverted thinking bestows upon them, they are more than willing to run things and will decidedly get things done; they are results-oriented. Above all else, ESTJs are responsible. Not only are they *ready* to take on responsibility, they *must* take on responsibility. Accountability is of great import to them, both their own and that of others. As they move to complete projects, they tend to be more task-focused than people-focused.

Sensing orients ESTJs to the present and to the facts, and thus their thinking is both logical and pragmatic. Their preference for sensing gives them a more hands-on approach to life, and they look to the utility of ideas and things. Sensing provides support to the dominant thinking by keeping ESTJs open to new facts, but the dominant force for them is still their drive to analyze and to make logical sense of things.

If ESTJs had a motto, it might be "just do it, and do it right." They have a great respect for the bottom line. And get to the bottom line, they will. ESTJs tend to be industrious people who have a strong work ethic. They value the fulfilling of duty, and if they have taken on a job, it will be completed. Realistic and precise, they attend to detail in bringing projects to fruition. The facts and figures will tell whether the project is done to satisfaction.

ESTJs form much of the backbone of society, and they feel that societal structures are the glue that maintains civilization. Thus, they give weight to institutional and community goals and expectations, and they strive to fulfill their obligations to those groups. They are pillars of the community and respect law and order; ESTJs are conscientious. Needless to say, they tend to be keepers of tradition. Holidays and birthdays, for example, are rigorously adhered to and celebrated. ESTJs appreciate the need for continuity and consistency in life, and thus they tend to value stability and security. If something has worked before, then it doesn't need to be changed— so notes their pragmatism.

ESTJs tend to be acutely aware of hierarchy, power, and authority. Position is earned through application and responsible action, and a person who has fulfilled these obligations competently is to be respected. Competence, in themselves and in others, is a thing to be prized. ESTJs often rise to positions of responsibility whatever their area, and so frequently are managers and executives.

They are very often found in business, banking, construction, the military, and politics, as well as many other areas where hands-on efficiency, analysis, and responsible action are required.

ESTJs are usually quite matter-of-fact in their interactions with others. They are confident, direct, and typically tough-minded. Because they want clarity, and because their dominant thinking gives them a sense of certainty in their reasoning and conclusions, ESTJs are usually quite comfortable issuing directives to get something done. This style can work well in business but can backfire in one's personal life. ESTJs consider it essential to treat people fairly, but paradoxically their certainty about what is correct can lead to their making decisions for others. Since they may also have difficulty listening to perspectives and observations that oppose their own, they may at times be seen as autocratic.

Without development of introverted sensing, ESTJs may rush to closure, making decisions too quickly without pausing to gather enough factual information. As a result they can appear inflexible, closed to input, and all too willing to make decisions just for the sake of getting things settled. Development of sensing will help them stay open to new information and avoid these traps. Also, development of intuition will help them see the longer term consequences of some of the decisions they make. With their task orientation and drive to increase efficiency, ESTJs can miss the human factor in getting things done. Thus, they may be seen as critical and impatient. Development of feeling will help them see the importance of attending not only to what they themselves care about, but to others' feelings and needs for appreciation.

Under stress ESTJs may become hypercritical, both of themselves and of others. They may feel unappreciated or may hear innocent comments as personal attacks. Under great stress, ESTJs may also become angry and controlling, issuing directives without attention to the consequences to other people. In the extreme, and in contrast to their usual outgoing and tough-minded style, they may feel trapped and alone, and even have out-of-proportion explosions of emotion.

Key words

active organizer ■ logical ■ facts ■ analytical

manage ■ pragmatic ■ productive ■ responsible ■ tough-minded

ESFJ
Extraverted Feeling with
Introverted Sensing

For ESFJs the dominant quality in their lives is an active and intense caring about people and a strong desire to bring harmony into their relationships. ESFJs bring an aura of warmth to all that they do, and they naturally move into action to help others, to organize the world around them, and to get things done. Sensing orients their feeling to current facts and realities, and thus gives their feeling a hands-on pragmatic quality. ESFJs take their work seriously and believe others should do so as well.

ESFJs are decisive because they are clear about what they value; they are clear about what is right and wrong, and what is good or bad. ESFJs want and expect the world to function harmoniously and in accord with the values and standards they feel are inherent in the natural order of things. Thus, they are comfortable using their dominant feeling to bring order to the outer world of people, events, and things. They are organizers who naturally move into action to give structure and to get things done.

ESFJs have an aura of warmth and friendliness that is easily felt by those around them. Openly expressive, they wear their hearts on their sleeves. They want to know others, and they want others to know them; above all else, they are sociable. ESFJs are concerned and compassionate, and their caring is not only intense, but *active* as well. They reach out to nurture others because they understand that helping is one of the highest goods in life. Their empathy cannot sit quietly. It translates immediately into energetic support and generous attention to the welfare of others.

ESFJs strive to develop harmony in their relationships. Harmony is *essential* to their well-being, and one way it is evident is in their appreciation of cooperation. ESFJs are not only cooperative themselves but win the cooperation of others through their enthusiastic warmth and helpfulness. Since relationships are of great importance to them, confrontations that may lead to hard feelings can be difficult for them to initiate. Their concern for harmony may also show itself as an avoidance of conflict, which can lead to a painful trap for ESFJs. They want harmony, but they also want above all else to do the right thing, two goals which are not always compatible. Sometimes doing the right thing means others may feel hurt, a conflict ESFJs eventually face as they mature.

Sensing orients ESFJs to the present and to the facts, and thus their style is both caring and pragmatic. Their preference for sensing gives them a hands-on approach to life, and they look for what *works*. They are typically not great lovers of theory, preferring rather to be actively involved in real life and to have the actual experience. Sensing gives ESFJs a realistic down-to-earth quality, and makes them look precise in their structuring of their lives. Sensing also provides support to the dominant feeling by keeping them open to new facts, but the dominant force for them is still their desire to actively bring the outer world into harmony with their intensely felt people-values.

ESFJs are responsible and dependable; they take their jobs seriously. They have a strong sense of duty and are thorough in their follow-through. They will do what needs to be done. This ethic arises out of a concern for carrying their fair share of the group's work. ESFJs feel accountable to the group, because they appreciate the need for people to be able to work together well.

Traditions are of great importance to ESFJs, who guard and protect customs and celebrations great and small. Anniversaries, birthdays, and holidays are enthusiastically observed and regarded. Stability and continuity are appreciated by ESFJs, who know that social structures help ease the chaos that exists in society. Often upholders of the customs and standards of the culture or community, they strive to create and preserve structure, both at home and at work. As hosts, hostesses, and caretakers, ESFJs help smooth the bumps of everyday life by ensuring the necessities are taken care of and people's needs are attended to in very practical ways. They are skilled at providing a warm, safe, and nurturing environment. Needless to say, family is *very* important to them.

The ESFJs' outgoing warmth can also find expression in the careers they often choose, careers where they can actively work with people, particularly in a hands-on or pragmatic way. ESFJs are often found in business, hands-on health care, education (particularly K-12), religious, and service careers. They can be comfortable in the leadership role and will delegate as necessary.

Relationships are very important to ESFJs. They seek active involvement with others, and they like to feel a sense of belonging. They readily express appreciation and they themselves like to be appreciated. Because feedback and affirmation are important to them, they may be easily hurt by criticism or indifference. With good development, ESFJs can be exquisitely sensitive to others; they have good communication skills and are usually quite tactful. Though they are usually seen as caring, ESFJs may at times be seen as intolerant and unwilling to listen to others, behavior that can arise from their strong sense of right and wrong. They may even make decisions for others that they feel are in that person's best interest and become impatient if others don't see the correctness of the action taken. Of course, others may be offended by this presumption, and as a result ESFJs can be seen as controlling or overbearing.

Without development of introverted sensing, ESFJs may rush to closure, jumping to conclusions too quickly without pausing to gather enough factual information. Development of sensing will help them stay open to new information, particularly about people. ESFJs can have too many "shoulds," which may lead to excessive amounts of guilt or to their being perceived as inflexible. Alternatively, in their desire to maintain harmony, their own personal needs may sometimes go unmet, as they respond too readily to what others think or feel. Development of intuition and thinking will help them address the worst of these difficulties. Thinking will help them learn to acknowledge both positives *and* negatives about themselves and others. Development of thinking can also help them solve rather than ignore or feel trapped by problems. Intuition and thinking will also help ESFJs see the longer range consequences of their actions, and to be open to new ways of doing things.

Under stress ESFJs can become overindulgent and excessively emotional. They may also have difficulty thinking clearly and thus see or imagine only the negative possibilities in a situation. In addition, they may become excessively sensitive and overly personalize comments made by others. Under extreme stress, ESFJs may become exceptionally critical of both themselves and of others.

Key words

warm ■ concerned ■ caring ■ enthusiastic

empathic ■ harmony ■ responsible ■ energetic ■ pragmatic ■ organize

ENFJ
Extraverted Feeling with
Introverted Intuition

For ENFJs the dominant quality in their lives is an active and intense caring about people and a strong desire to bring harmony into their relationships. ENFJs are openly expressive and empathic people who bring an aura of warmth to all that they do. Intuition orients their feeling to the new and to the possible, thus they often enjoy working to manifest a humanitarian vision, or helping others develop their potential. ENFJs naturally and conscientiously move into action to care for others, to organize the world around them, and to get things done.

ENFJs love opportunities to talk with and learn from others, and derive great joy and energy from diving right into the sea of relationships that make up our world. To ENFJs, people are what the world is about. They are warm, enthusiastic, and optimistic people who have a wide range of friends and an active social life. Their sociability is not quiet, but very expressive and fun-loving, and they wear their hearts on their sleeves.

ENFJs tend also to have exceptional people skills. At their best, they are compassionate and exquisitely sensitive to the feelings and needs of others, and they energetically respond to those needs. ENFJs strive to establish harmony in their relationships, one expression of which is their bias toward cooperation. They are not only cooperative themselves, but win cooperation from others through their empathy and warm caring. Their concern with harmony may at times, however, manifest itself as an avoidance of conflict.

ENFJs make decisions based on personal values and on their very clear sense of right and wrong, which they usually share openly. Conclusions about people are often drawn quickly and with certainty. When an ENFJ decides a person is trustworthy and good, it is a difficult conclusion to dispel; ENFJs prize and embody loyalty. However, it is equally difficult for them to dispel negative conclusions they may draw. They can also at times be frustrated by those who are not as quick to decide and to act as are they.

Intuition orients ENFJs to the future, to possibilities, and to patterns, thus their style is both caring and imaginative. They are creative folks who enjoy planning, and they are especially excited by "possibilities for people." Their preference for intuition also gives them a more conceptual and global approach to life. Intuition provides support to dominant feeling by keeping them open to new information, but the dominant force for ENFJs is still their desire to actively bring the outer world into harmony with their intensely felt people-values.

As a rule, ENFJs are responsible people who like to get things settled and who are conscientious in following through on commitments. They like to be involved in many things at once and often pull it off because they are organized. ENFJs can be particularly skillful in energizing people and orchestrating activities to achieve a vision. They are most deeply moved by causes that feed, nurture, and support people, and they have endless energy for work that fulfills their humanitarian values.

ENFJs are skilled communicators; they are often masters of the spoken word, but they may be quite skilled writers as well. Their thought is symbolic and metaphorical, and they look for meaning in everything. They revel in accounts of human events and relationships, as found in the theater, in cinema, and in writing, perhaps enjoying the active forms more so than the written. In their curiosity about ideas, they often enjoy school, particularly the humanities and arts. Since ENFJs value creativity, and they often have strong needs for freedom of expression, they are commonly found in careers in the performing and fine arts.

ENFJs are idealists who want and need active people contact in their careers. They orient naturally to the positive in people, and they want to help others manifest their potential. Often deeply concerned with the emotional and spiritual life, they are frequently found in careers where they can attend to issues of growth and human development. Since they look for meanings in words, actions, and events, ENFJs can have acute insight into people. They are often group catalysts and may be inspiring and persuasive healers, teachers, motivators, and leaders. ENFJs issue directives naturally, which they see as a way of facilitating group process; with business interests and with their orientation to the future, they can be insightful marketers and natural planners.

In relationships, ENFJs are friendly, energetic, and emotionally expressive. They exude charm, but may also overwhelm others through too much enthusiasm. Typically generous and hospitable folks, they also value genuineness in their relationships. Though ENFJs can be very tactful, they may at times be experienced as manipulative. They certainly do not intend to be, but their clear perception of "the good" can lead them to make decisions for others and to push others toward what the ENFJ perceives to be the best for that person.

Another danger for ENFJs is that they may inadvertently take on the concerns and responsibilities of others, and in their desire for harmony their own needs may not get met. They express appreciation naturally, and they thrive on both recognition and appreciation; as a result ENFJs tend to be hurt by indifference. They are very much turned off by criticism and cool logic.

For ENFJs, there is often a certainty in their conclusions about what is the good and right action. Development of introverted intuition will help them stay open to new information, particularly about people, and also help them avoid some of the pitfalls of this certainty. With their idealism, ENFJs can have unrealistic expectations about relationships, and they may have too many "shoulds." Development of intuition will keep them open to others' ideas, and help them listen to what others have to say. Development of sensing will help them see things as they are, and ways to work out their dreams in the practical world. ENFJs can also grow from learning to acknowledge unpleasant facts about themselves and others, and from learning to solve rather than ignore problems, a skill that will come with development of their thinking.

Under stress, ENFJs can become rigidly narrow in their perceptions, and become extremely emotional and generally irritable. They may doubt themselves and their abilities, and indiscriminately seek help or advice from others. Under great stress, ENFJs can become exceptionally critical of themselves and in contrast to their usual concern for appreciation and harmony, they can become decidedly critical of others.

Key words

warmth ■ enthusiasm ■ harmony
vision ■ active ■ cooperation ■ ideals ■ catalyst ■ communicate

ENTJ
Extraverted Thinking with Introverted Intuition

For ENTJs the driving force in their lives is their need to analyze and bring into logical order the outer world of events, people, and things. ENTJs are natural leaders who build conceptual models that serve as plans for strategic action. Intuition orients their thinking to the future, and gives their thinking an abstract quality. ENTJs will actively pursue and direct others in the pursuit of goals they have set, and they prefer a world that is structured and organized.

For ENTJs logic and analysis are paramount. They believe the outer world should and will make sense, and they strive to bring that world into logical order. Energetic and decisive, ENTJs literally drive toward closure in the outer world, and they naturally push organizations and the people in them to be more effective. They abhor disorganized activity and live for decisions; it feels good to them to settle things and move onward. ENTJs would rather be certain and be wrong than be uncertain.

ENTJs have very clear standards about what constitutes right and wrong, correct and incorrect behavior, and they are usually open in their critique of what goes on around them. They are natural skeptics and will spontaneously question anything that comes into their purview. With their sense of certainty, ENTJs are decidedly willing to take on responsibility and will quickly take the initiative to bring order out of chaos. They are movers and shakers, becoming excited by an idea and enthusiastically working to find an application for it.

Intuition orients ENTJs to meanings, patterns, and the big picture, and thus their thinking is both logical and abstract. Intuition's orientation to possibilities also makes their thinking creative and futuristic. Intuition provides support to dominant thinking by keeping ENTJs open to new information and new possibilities, but the dominant force for them is still a drive to analyze and to make logical sense of things.

ENTJs are energetic planners and builders, projecting themselves into the future with ease. As complex and critical thinkers, they naturally find logical flaws and inconsistencies in what is said or done, and are at home analyzing what will or won't work in a plan. Since ENTJs strategically analyze alternatives and possible outcomes, they believe, and easily convince others, that they have the wherewithal to make the future happen now. The truth is that they usually *will* make it happen; they will set a goal and achieve it at all costs. As a result, ENTJs are often found in leadership positions.

ENTJs are intellectually curious and love exploring new ideas. They like to exercise their ingenuity in solving problems and in addressing challenges. In spite of their love of mental models, their drive for closure in the outer world does tend to make them pragmatic. Above all, ENTJs want to be "effective" and like to demonstrate it. They want the world to run efficiently and planfully, but may themselves be intolerant of routine and may prefer to leave follow-through on plans and projects to others.

ENTJs deeply value competence and intelligence, both in themselves and in others. They set high goals, and continually hold themselves to an exceptionally high (possibly too high at times) standard of accomplishment. ENTJs value achievement and want to be recognized for what they have done. They are strong believers in the power of the will, assuming that with the correct application of willpower, anything can be accomplished. ENTJs also deeply value autonomy, and they are often acutely aware of status and power issues.

ENTJs are often found in the fields of science and technology, but are also found in teaching, law, business, and the military. Typically, they are found in executive, administrative, and leadership positions, whatever their field.

ENTJs are usually quite frank and straightforward in their interactions with others. They are confident and assertive, and can take a clear stand and maintain it in the face of dissent. ENTJs will not be bound by rules or expectations imposed by others. Interestingly, they may be or appear to be all too willing to make decisions for others. Though rules may be seen as practical necessities, their inherent skepticism won't let them follow structures without question. If they see a better way, and they often do, ENTJs will drive their way to the top in order to redefine the rules. If they appear to hold themselves in high regard at times, it is only because they are certain of the correctness of their logic and insightful analyses, and are willing to outwardly express their certainty.

ENTJs deeply value justice, and they consider it essential to treat others fairly. Paradoxically, in their drive to be fair, they may come across as cool and impersonal. In the extreme, they can appear arrogant, critical, and argumentative. They may even overwhelm others with their drive and decisiveness. ENTJs may indeed be insensitive at times to interpersonal issues and the needs of others, particularly others' needs for appreciation or recognition.

Without development of introverted intuition, ENTJs can rush to closure, making decisions without pausing to gather enough information and without exploring possible alternatives. Thus, they may appear rigid and closed to input. Development of intuition will help them stay open to new information. Since ENTJs can be bored with the literal working out of plans, development of sensing will help them have a healthy respect for the details necessary to turn plans into realities. Development of feeling will benefit ENTJs in a number of ways, including helping them be more tolerant of the perceived incompetence or inefficiency of others, and of themselves. Such development would also help them give greater attention to the human aspects of situations, including how others and they themselves feel.

Under stress ENTJs may become hypercritical of themselves and of others. They may also become angry and controlling, issuing directives without attention to the consequences or the impact of their behavior on other people. Under extreme stress, and in contrast to their usually active and logical style, they may feel trapped, overemotional, and alone, or may even hear innocent comments as personal attacks.

Key words

driving ■ leader ■ planner ■ vision ■ organizer

strategic ■ systems ■ tough-minded ■ logic ■ analysis ■ patterns ■ competence

How Frequent Is My Type?

One of the common questions people ask after *determining* their type is: How *frequent* is my type? Table Two shows estimates of the relative frequency of each of the sixteen types in the United States population. The symbols on the type table represent percentages of the general population. This means you can "eyeball" the table and detect the relative frequency of your type.

Looking at Table Two you can see that the weight of the table lies across the bottom two rows and in the left two columns. The intersection of these two rows and two columns in the bottom left quadrant represents the highest concentration of the general population. Most data suggest that extraverted types and sensing types are relatively more frequent than introverted types and intuitive types.

In fact, the four types combining E and S represent about 35-40% of the U.S. population. The general U.S. population is primarily composed of action-oriented pragmatists who value the proven and the known and who want to see results.

While most ES types probably found many other people like themselves as they grew up, their counterpart types, the introverts with intuition (INs), were less likely to find people like themselves. This is because the data suggest INs represent about 15-20% of the U.S. population. These less frequent, reflective, and imaginative types enjoy innovation in the world of ideas.

One consequence of being a less frequent type is that these individuals report as young people having had more difficulty finding kindred spirits among their classmates. Interestingly, because of career choice patterns, the percentage of IN teachers increases as grade level increases. So the ES students, while in the majority, will find fewer and fewer teachers like themselves as they advance through the grades. In contrast, the less frequent IN students will find more teachers like themselves as they advance. Overall, the types least likely to find teachers who appreciate their adaptable hands-on learning style are the four SP types. You can explore this issue for yourself by examining Table Three, which shows the frequencies of teachers at different levels of education.

As each of the types leave high school to work or to pursue higher education, we begin to see differences in the frequencies of the types that are attracted to work and to school. The practical and active ES types are much more likely to enter the world of work and pursue jobs in business and industry. In contrast, the reflective and theory-oriented IN types tend to pursue college and advanced degrees, and are more often found in careers in education, the sciences, and the humanities. Although these patterns generally hold true, it is important to understand that every type is found at every level of education and in virtually every career. More information on type and careers can be found in the last section of this book.

Will My Type Change?

Another question often asked is: Will my type change? Research on type and on other measures of personality shows that our character is reasonably stable over time. As we grow, our personality traits are more likely to mature rather than to change into something different. In type terms this means we develop more sophistication with our primary preferences while expanding our abilities in our nonpreferences. In short, our type stays the same, but we develop a wider range of skills.

Some people do, however, report different type preferences at different times when taking the MBTI. Why? Although the Indicator is very reliable, it is not a perfect tool and is subject to error. This is why the person who gives you the Indicator takes such care to explain the results and to verify their accuracy with you. The goal is to assess and verify your *true* type.

If you believe your results from the Indicator are not accurate, remember that a number of things could influence the measurement of your type.

One possible influence is social expectation. You may have answered based on how

Table Two

Estimated Frequencies of the Types in the United States Population

	Sensing		Intuition	
	Thinking	Feeling	Feeling	Thinking
Introversion **Judgment**	**ISTJ** 12–16% ▪▪▪▪▪▪▪▪▪▪▪▪ ▪▪▪▪	**ISFJ** 10–13% ▪▪▪▪▪▪▪▪▪▪▪▪ ▪	**INFJ** 2–3% ▪▪	**INTJ** 3–4% ▪▪▪
Perception	**ISTP** 5–7% ▪▪▪▪▪▪	**ISFP** 5–7% ▪▪▪▪▪▪	**INFP** 4–5% ▪▪▪▪	**INTP** 5–6% ▪▪▪▪▪
Extraversion **Perception**	**ESTP** 5–7% ▪▪▪▪▪▪	**ESFP** 6–9% ▪▪▪▪▪▪▪	**ENFP** 6–8% ▪▪▪▪▪▪▪	**ENTP** 4–7% ▪▪▪▪▪
Judgment	**ESTJ** 10–12% ▪▪▪▪▪▪▪▪▪▪ ▪	**ESFJ** 10–12% ▪▪▪▪▪▪▪▪▪▪ ▪	**ENFJ** 3–5% ▪▪▪▪	**ENTJ** 3–5% ▪▪▪▪

E 50–55%	I 45–50%		
S 65–70%	N 30–35%		
T 45–55%	F 45–55%		
J 55–60%	P 40–45%		

▪ = approximately one percent

you behave to meet social or familial expectations, rather than how you might naturally behave when you are being yourself. An example of this is the teenager who lives in a home where the family norm is eating quietly at the dinner table, and later reading quietly by one's self. If the teenager in this situation preferred extraversion, but reported these kinds of introverted behaviors when taking the Indicator, the results might show a preference for introversion.

Our jobs can influence our responses as well. Even though we are told there are no right or wrong answers on the Indicator, if we take it in the workplace, we may report responses we truly believe to be the "best" answers for our work setting.

Another possible influence arises when people feel they experience many of the negative aspects of their preferences, or when

they view the opposite preferences more positively. As a result, people may respond to the Indicator in ways that reflect their non-preferences because they wish they engaged in those behaviors more often. Psychological distress may influence results as well. In crisis or under great stress, we may change our behavior dramatically, and as a result, we may not get the most accurate assessment of our natural style.

If you believe any of these situations fit you, you may want to be cautious in interpreting your results. Take the time to clarify how social and work expectations or stress may be influencing the accuracy of your report.

The last reason that results may change is due to simple error. One time you may take the Indicator and answer one way and the next time you make just enough changes in

Table Three

Percentages of Teachers at Different Levels of Education

	ISTJ	ISFJ	INFJ	INTJ
Pre-school	3.0	20.0	7.0	4.0
Elementary	10.1	17.9	5.1	2.1
Middle & Jr.	11.7	12.2	5.0	4.5
High School	11.9	10.6	7.7	5.4
University	12.8	6.1	7.5	10.9

	ISTP	ISFP	INFP	INTP
Pre-school	0.0	4.0	8.0	2.0
Elementary	1.7	4.7	4.6	1.5
Middle & Jr.	2.3	3.2	5.9	2.4
High School	1.5	2.5	6.3	2.9
University	1.7	1.7	8.1	5.4

	ESTP	ESFP	ENFP	ENTP
Pre-school	0.0	8.0	12.0	1.0
Elementary	0.9	5.7	10.2	1.5
Middle & Jr.	1.8	3.8	10.1	3.9
High School	1.1	2.3	11.4	3.5
University	1.2	1.7	9.1	5.3

	ESTJ	ESFJ	ENFJ	ENTJ
Pre-school	6.0	12.0	8.0	5.0
Elementary	8.5	12.4	7.2	5.2
Middle & Jr.	9.1	11.5	7.8	4.3
High School	11.3	8.5	8.8	4.3
University	6.5	4.4	8.0	9.6

Note: Numbers preceding bar graphs represent the percent of the sample falling in that type.

your answers to throw you in a different direction on one or more of the scales.

All of these are reasons why the practitioner takes such care to explain and verify the results with you. This is also why it is important to avoid guessing someone's type from just one behavior. If a scientifically validated measure asking many questions can be in error, then people asking one question can easily be wrong.

All the possible sources of inaccuracy mentioned are helpful in understanding how we may have mis-reported our type. They are also issues the authors of the Indicator had to tackle to create a reliable measurement tool, and it makes sense to interpret the results with these issues in mind. The fact, however, is that the Indicator *is* accurate most of the time and is an excellent tool for helping people determine their type.

Applications of Type

So what is the point of all of this? What does type mean for our everyday lives? The MBTI was originally developed to help people gain a better understanding of themselves and a better understanding and appreciation of others. In this way it was hoped that people could learn how to make constructive use of the natural differences that exist among individuals. Throughout the long years of the Indicator's development, type has been applied in an ever increasing number of ways, all with the above ends in mind. This section is an overview of the different ways type is currently being used and applied in everyday life.

Since type is all about learning about one's self and learning about others, it has applications in any area in which people are involved with one another. And that is quite a broad scope!

Understanding and appreciating ourselves. Many people find type is a useful way of understanding themselves and how they respond to the circumstances in their lives. Type can help individuals develop acceptance of themselves and an appreciation of their own likes, needs, or developmental paths. Many people upon their first introduction to type say, "Oh, that's why I like these things, don't like these other things, and why I behave this way at work and at home." Through a knowledge of type you can have a better understanding of your need for privacy or need for activity, your need for hands-on versus book learning, and so on. An appreciation of your own natural strengths and pitfalls is a big step toward self-esteem and growth.

Understanding and appreciating others. Since most of us live in a world populated by other people, we are always involved in relationships. Whether those relationships are with acquaintances, coworkers, or significant others, we often find that other people have very different type preferences from our own. Since each type has its own strengths and potential blindspots, we can see the importance of having a variety of types in the world who are involved in many different kinds of activities.

The different types can complement each other because each brings a valuable perspective to any activity. Sensing types provide a pragmatic realism, while intuitive types provide a view of the possibilities. Thinking types provide an impersonal analysis of the situation, while feeling types provide a look at the personal and human consequences of an action. When we realize that each type has something valuable to offer, and that people act in ways that are natural extensions of their type preferences, we are less likely to see differences as personal affronts. We are also more likely to understand that someone of another type provides a perspective on a situation that we may be missing.

As we appreciate that type differences are very real, at least two opportunities for growth present themselves. First, we can see our potential blindspots and go on to develop our own less preferred functions. And second, we can learn to value the differences that others bring to our lives, and we can learn to seek the input of others who have that complementary perspective. The table below describes a few of the many things the different types have to offer each other.

What the Types Can Offer Each Other

Extraverts

- Provide the outwardly directed energy needed to move into action.

- Offer responsiveness to what is going on in the environment.

- Have a natural inclination to converse and to network.

Introverts

- Provide the inwardly directed energy needed for focused reflection.

- Offer stability from attending to enduring ideas.

- Have a natural tendency to think and work alone.

Sensing types

- Have a mastery of the facts.

- Bring a knowledge of what materials and resources are available.

- Appreciate knowing and doing what works.

Intuitive types

- Know by way of insight and attention to meanings.

- Bring a grasp of what is possible and what the trends are.

- Appreciate doing what hasn't been tried before.

Thinking types

- Take a hard look at the pros and cons of situations, even when they have a personal stake.

- Have an ability to analyze and solve problems.

- Want to discover the "truth" and they naturally notice logical inconsistencies.

Feeling types

- Know what is important to and for people, and adhere to that in the face of opposition.

- Have an ability to build relationships and to be persuasive.

- Want to uncover the greatest "good" in a situation and they notice when people may be harmed.

Judging types

- Can organize, plan, and follow through on projects.

- Push to get things settled and decided.

- Appreciate well-oiled efficiency at work.

Perceiving types

- Can respond quickly and flexibly to the needs of the moment.

- Strive to keep things open so new information may be gathered.

- Appreciate the need for spontaneity and exploration at work.

Relationships

Type differences in relationships can be a source of growth and/or conflict. However, there are no best or more successful combinations of types in relationships. Certainly two persons who share all four preferences can be in continual conflict, while another couple who share only one or two preferences may experience relatively little conflict. When there *is* conflict in a relationship it is often around issues that arise from type differences. For example, one partner may be more interested in spending time alone or with just the partner, while the other partner may feel the need to spend time with a larger number of people. These are differences that can be either a source of frustration or opportunities to learn and grow from one another.

Knowledge of type not only helps us better understand others but also helps us learn ways of communicating with those of different type preferences. That is, we can learn to talk more "in type." For example, when talking with an intuitive, we can remember that first discussing the big picture and the possibilities will more likely lead to the intuitive's feeling understood, and lead more quickly to a sense of rapport. For further reading on type and relationships, you may want to read *Intimacy and Type* or some of the other materials listed in the final *Resources* section of this book.

Careers

Research has clearly shown that people are attracted to those careers that allow them to make use of their natural type preferences.

Though all four letters of your type can affect the kind of career that interests you, the two middle letters (ST, SF, NF, or NT) of your type have a particular importance for your career choice. That is, your combination of perception (sensing or intuition) and judgment (thinking or feeling) seems to have the most influence on which kinds of careers will attract you. In the table to the right, you can see the effects these combinations may have.

Type can provide you with useful information on a variety of issues related to career choice. For example, your preference for extraversion or introversion may tell you how much need you have for ongoing (E) versus more limited (I) interactions with others. Your preference for judging versus perceiving can tell you how organized (J) or flexible (P) your job search is likely to be, as well as how much or how little structure you might like in your job (J or P).

There is more to an individual than his or her type preferences. So when you make career decisions you will want more information about yourself in addition to knowledge of your type. For a more in-depth look at type and careers, see *Looking at Type and Careers* or some of the other materials listed in the final *Resources* section of this book.

Education

Type can also tell us things about the way people prefer to learn. For example, persons with a preference for extraversion often prefer learning situations that allow them to talk with others and to become physically engaged with the environment. Those with a preference for introversion often prefer learning environments that allow them to engage in quiet reflection and where they can keep their thoughts inside until they are well developed. The table below shows some of the other effects type may have on preferences for learning.

An understanding of type leads to the appreciation that there are many different and equally valuable ways to learn. Type can also help you identify what some of your strengths and pitfalls might be as you approach studying and learning. For more information about

Sensing plus Thinking (ST)

STs tend to approach life and work in an objective and analytical manner, and like to focus on realities and practical applications in their work. They are often found in careers that require a technical approach to things, ideas, or people, and tend to be less interested in careers that require nurturing of others or attending to their growth and development. STs are often found in careers in business, management, banking, applied sciences, construction, production, police, and the military.

Sensing plus Feeling (SF)

SFs tend to approach life and work in a warm and people-oriented manner, and like to focus on realities and hands-on kinds of careers. They are often found in human services and in careers that require a sympathetic approach to people, and tend to be less interested in careers that require an analytical and impersonal approach to information and ideas. SFs are often found in careers in the clergy, teaching, health care, child care, sales and office work, and personal services.

Intuition plus Feeling (NF)

NFs tend to approach life and work in a warm and enthusiastic manner, and like to focus on ideas and possibilities, particularly "possibilities for people." They are often found in careers that require communication skills, a focus on the abstract, and an understanding of others. They tend to be less interested in careers that require an impersonal or technical approach to things and factual data. NFs are often found in careers in the arts, the clergy, counseling and psychology, writing, education, research, and health care.

Intuition plus Thinking (NT)

NTs tend to approach life and work in a logical and objective manner, and like to make use of their ingenuity to focus on possibilities, particularly possibilities that have a technical application. They are often found in careers that require an impersonal and analytical approach to ideas, information and people, and they tend to be less interested in careers that require a warm, sympathetic and hands-on approach to helping people. NTs are often found in careers in the sciences, law, computers, the arts, engineering, management, and technical work.

type, education, and learning, see *People Types and Tiger Stripes*, or some of the other materials listed in the *Resources* section of this book.

Extraversion

May prefer learning through discussion or working with groups

Sensing

May prefer learning tasks that require observing for specifics or memory for facts

Thinking

May learn better when the teacher logically organizes material

Judging

May prefer studying and learning in a more steady and orderly way with a drive to closure

Introversion

May prefer learning through reading or working individually

Intuition

May prefer learning tasks that call for imagination or attention to general concepts

Feeling

May learn better when they feel they have a personal rapport with the teacher

Perceiving

May prefer studying and learning in a more flexible and informal way with an orientation to discovery

Spirituality

Many people find type provides a way of understanding their spiritual path and development: their natural gifts as well as potential blindspots. Several writers have noted that different types are drawn to different spiritual practices and have different ways of expressing their understandings of spirituality. Introverts, for example, might be more drawn to solitary or reflective practices, while extraverts might be more drawn to group or active spiritual practices. Other writers have talked about the spiritual gifts associated with the different attitudes and functions. For example, sensing carries the gifts of practicality and simplicity, intuition the gifts of vision and insight, thinking the gifts of planning and justice, and feeling the gifts of caring and compassion.

The path of type development has been viewed by many writers as a helpful map for understanding aspects of an individual's spiritual development as well. The priority each type gives the mental functions can also be seen as the order in which that type is most likely to develop them (see Table One in this book), with the development of each function bringing new spiritual challenges and gifts. For more extended discussions of type and spirituality, you may want to see *God's Gifted*

People or some of the other materials listed in the *Resources* section of this book.

Work/Organizations

Type is widely used in work and organizational settings. As we have already noted, different types are clearly drawn to different careers. However, within any given job or work setting, the tasks are usually varied enough that we will find many different types represented in that setting. This diversity in types can be healthy and stimulating, but can also lead to misunderstandings and frictions in the workplace. Type can be useful in work and organizational settings in a number of ways:

■ to help individuals see that different approaches to working and problem solving can be of benefit to the organization rather than a source of friction

■ to improve communication between persons who work in the organization

■ to build effective teams

■ to solve problems and resolve conflict

■ to better understand and appreciate different leadership and management styles

There is an enormous amount of literature on the applications of type in organizational settings. You might want to start with

Looking at Type in the Workplace or some of the other materials listed in the *Resources* section of this book.

Counseling

Jung originally developed his theory of types as part of his counseling with his clients. Thus, we see that the core of type theory has its roots in the practice of psychological counseling, and type is still being used there today. Type can shed light on a number of issues commonly dealt with in counseling, including: self-esteem, relationship difficulties, life development and transitions, decision-making, and others. We have already seen how type can be applied to relationship issues. Type can also provide a nonthreatening way to talk about many different issues in counseling.

As we have said in this book, a balance of perception and judgment is important for healthy personality development. This understanding helps us see how difficulties may arise in a person's life depending on whether that person stays open to new information for too long, or whether that person comes to closure too often or too soon on issues.

You may find, for example, that if you have either sensing or intuition as your dominant function (see Table One on page 9 if you need a reminder), then coming to closure or settling on a decision may not be your strong point. You may not trust your ability to make good decisions. If either thinking or feeling is your dominant function, then staying open to new information or hearing new input may not be your strong point. You may feel certain about your decisions, but lack of new information may leave you feeling stuck—with no sense of other options that may be open to you. Counseling is a good place to explore these kinds of concerns, and an understanding of type can help you do it in a way that respects your individual differences.

For more information on how the different types may look under stress and also for some suggestions for type development, you may want to see *Beside Ourselves* or some of the other materials listed in the final *Resources* section of this book.

Problem Solving

Isabel Myers described a type-based method of problem solving that could be used by individuals or groups. Myers understood that in solving problems all four functions (sensing, intuition, thinking, feeling) are involved, and that people naturally tend to emphasize those functions that represent their preferences. Use of the model can help you see the strengths and pitfalls for your type as you go about solving problems, and in using it you may become aware of new information, and possibly draw some different conclusions. This model may be applied anywhere that information must be gathered and decisions made (as in business decisions, career exploration, or educational choices).

Myers referred to this problem-solving process as the "controlled use of perception and judgment." The four steps described below are a way of ensuring that all four functions are (ideally) brought into play. The process may also be viewed as a circle, and although people will naturally enter the circle at different points, the steps below can be a reminder to include all four components of the problem-solving process.

In this model you use your tools of perception (sensing and intuition) to see all aspects of your situation, and you use your tools of judgment (thinking and feeling) to make decisions based on both impersonal and personal criteria. The key here is to use each of the functions as best you can without letting the others get in the way at that step in the problem-solving process. In this way all the bases get covered. Below are some questions and statements that can help you engage each function as you go through the problem-solving process.

Step One: Sensing Perception

You use sensing to determine the facts, data, and givens in a situation, and to face the realities of whatever issue is before you. What, exactly, is the current situation? What is the history of the situation? What assets and liabilities do you or others bring to the situation and what resources are actually available? What does an impartial look at the problem tell you, and what are the practical issues?

Step Two: Intuitive Perception

You use intuition to look at the possibilities in a situation, ways to change a situation, and to notice meanings and patterns in whatever issue is before you. What does this situation mean in the context of your life (or business, or whatever) and your future? For example, where do you want to be in five years? Can you brainstorm new ways of approaching the issue, even seemingly outrageous ways, without censoring any of them? Are there ideas that make no sense but are difficult to discount?

Step Three: Thinking Judgment

You use thinking to make a critical and impersonal analysis of the situation, of the facts and possibilities you discovered in the first two steps. Look at the logical consequences (both positive and negative) of acting on the various choices you have available to you, particularly the ones that are most attractive to you. If you step outside of yourself and the situation, what do you see objectively and critically about yourself and about the situation?

Step Four: Feeling Judgment

You use feeling to weigh how much you care about the possible outcomes of the different options, to determine what each choice means to you personally, and to look at the people consequences of any decisions. With feeling you give weight to your personal values, to what is important to you. What do you really care about in the long run, even if it seems "illogical" to care about those things? You also use feeling to weigh what impact a decision may have on the feelings and values of others.

Once you have worked through these different steps, you can make a decision that is more informed, move into action on your decision, and then evaluate the outcome of your action. At that point, you may be happy with your decision. If you are not, you can go through the four steps again, perhaps with greater emphasis on the steps to which you may have given less time.

Not surprisingly, people tend to focus on the two steps that reflect the two middle letters of their four-letter type. Again, Table One indicates the priority each of the sixteen types gives the four mental functions. In theory, you will tend to spend less time on the steps of the problem-solving process that require you to use your third and fourth functions. Thus, consciously working through all four steps may require some effort, but will lead to more informed problem solving. Whether working alone or in a group, discussion with another type can be helpful to provide "constructive use of differences." Someone with type preferences different from our own can provide us with the perspective we most need to be a more effective problem-solver.

For more in-depth information on type and problem solving, you may want to see *People Types and Tiger Stripes* or some of the other materials listed in the final *Resources* section of this book.

Learning More About Type

There are many excellent resources for learning more about type. You can read some of the other books described in the final *Resources* section of this book, and also become involved with the organizations that provide type training, membership services, and materials on psychological type.

As you continue to use type, you will find that your understanding of it becomes more sophisticated and you will develop an even greater appreciation of its complexity and the variety of ways in which it can be applied. People will often go through four broad stages of understanding* as they use their new-found type knowledge.

The first stage is: "*Wow,* isn't this exciting?! You and I are different, and type really explains a lot about our differences." Often people are fascinated by how a simple questionnaire can capture so much information about themselves. This first stage of understanding reflects that sense of wonder.

After learning about type and observing yourself and others for a time, a very natural second stage of self-appreciation emerges. At this point you *may* become caught up in the strengths of your own type preferences. You might find yourself saying, "*Heh-heh!!* I know they said no type is really better than any of the others, but my type really does seem to be very good."

In the third stage, you may become more aware of type-related areas where you have less skill or comfort. The hazard is that you may minimize the importance of doing activities associated with your nonpreferences. For example, you may find yourself saying, "*So that means* I don't do this or that (e.g., people skills, make plans) well. It's not my strength. I leave those things for others." Type can explain why certain activities may be difficult for you, but type is *not* an excuse for avoiding responsibility or for dodging tasks that are rightly yours.

The fourth and final stage is one of perspective. It is characterized by "*Ahh,* I recognize the strengths that other types bring. I see the power that comes from multiple types tackling problems, and I have a true appreciation of the constructive use of differences."

Of course people don't necessarily pass through these stages in a lock-step fashion, or finish with them once and for all. Knowing these stages, however, can provide us with a helpful way of testing our understanding of type. People newly introduced to type do often confront these issues and may pass through the stages many times. The *Ahh* stage is much more elusive than it first appears. We can sometimes believe we are more capable than we really are of using differences constructively! Learning to respect individual differences is not something that truly has an end; it is a learning that asks of us ongoing attention and a willingness to grow.

*Adapted from Susan Brock.

Further Resources

Books about type

Beside Ourselves by Naomi L. Quenk. Palo Alto, CA: Consulting Psychologists Press, Inc., 1993.

Gifts Differing by Isabel Briggs Myers with Peter B. Myers. Palo Alto, CA: Consulting Psychologists Press, Inc., 1980.

God's Gifted People by Gary L. Harbaugh. Minneapolis: Augsberg Publishing House, 1988.

Intimacy and Type by Jane Hardy Jones and Ruth G. Sherman. Gainesville, FL: Center for Applications of Psychological Type, 1997.

LifeTypes by Sandra Krebs Hirsh and Jean M. Kummerow. New York: Warner Books, 1989.

Looking at Type and Careers by Charles Martin. Gainesville, FL: Center for Applications of Psychological Type, 1995.

Looking at Type and Spirituality by Sandra Krebs Hirsh and Jane A.G. Kise. Gainesville, FL: Center for Applications of Psychological Type, 1997.

Looking at Type in the Workplace by Larry Demarest. Gainesville, FL: Center for Applications of Psychological Type, 1997.

People Types and Tiger Stripes (3rd edition) by Gordon D. Lawrence. Gainesville, FL: Center for Applications of Psychological Type, 1993.

Please Understand Me by David Keirsey and Marilyn Bates. Del Mar, CA: Prometheus Nemesis Book Co., 1984.

Type Talk by Otto Kroeger with Janet M. Thuesen. New York: Delacorte Press, 1988.

Work, Play, and Type by Judith Provost. Palo Alto, CA: Consulting Psychologists Press, Inc., 1990.

Books about Jung and his typology

Boundaries of the Soul by June Singer. New York: Doubleday, 1972.

Personality Types: Jung's Model of Typology by Daryl Sharp. Toronto, Canada: Inner City Books, 1987.

Background Notes

About the Publisher

The Center for Applications of Psychological Type, Inc. (CAPT) was established in the summer of 1975 with two major goals: to help make what is already known about psychological types useful in practical ways and to create new knowledge. Its founders, Isabel Briggs Myers and Mary H. McCaulley, adopted "the constructive use of differences" as the motto for this non-profit organization.

CAPT educates the public and professionals to view differences constructively by maintaining a number of services for use in education, counseling, organizational development, religious life, and research.

■ CAPT houses the Isabel Briggs Myers Memorial Library, the largest collection of MBTI publications, dissertations, and theses in the world. Research services are also available through the Library.

■ CAPT publishes and distributes papers and books related to research and practical applications of the Indicator. Ongoing research is conducted and made available through new products and services.

■ CAPT computer scoring for the MBTI produces high-quality, professional reports. This service attracts a large number of MBTI users; it also facilitates the collection of MBTI responses, contributing significantly to original research on the study of personality.

■ The Educational Department of CAPT offers basic and advanced training worldwide for managers, educators, counselors, psychotherapists, career counselors, psychologists, organizational development consultants, and religious leaders. CAPT has also sponsored and co-sponsored international conferences since 1975.

For a catalog about all these service and products, contact CAPT.

Center for Applications of
Psychological Type, Inc.
2815 N.W. 13th Street, Suite 401
Gainesville, FL 32609
(800) 777-2278
E-mail: capt@capt.org
Website: http://www.capt.org

About the Author

Charles Martin, Ph.D., is a licensed psychologist who uses type as a tool to help clients improve the quality of their lives and to help individuals and organizations enhance their performance. He is a consultant and trainer for the Center for Applications of Psychological Type and conducts MBTI qualifying programs and other MBTI training workshops nationally and internationally. He is also the author of a popular book on career planning, *Looking at Type and Careers*.

Notes